The Catholic Mass

Frits Albers Ph.B.

Edited by Frank Calneggia

En Route Books and Media, LLC
Saint Louis, MO

ENROUTE
Make the time

En Route Books and Media, LLC
5705 Rhodes Avenue
St. Louis, MO 63109

Cover credit: The Vision of the Most Holy Trinity and Our Lady of Fatima at Tuy, Spain, June 13, 1929, given to Ven. Sr. Lucia dos Santos

First Published October 1982
On the Feast of the Holy Rosary

ISBN-13: 979-8-88870-528-5
Library of Congress Control Number: 2026939349

Dedicated to
St. Pio of Pietrelcina (Padre Pio)

There is hardly a modern-day saint more appropriate than St Pio to whom to dedicate this marvellous book by Frits Albers on the Holy Sacrifice of the Mass. A number of biographies and good books have been written about him, to which I refer readers who want to learn more about this extraordinary saint who described himself simply as "a poor brother who prays". Here I confine myself to quoting from **(i)** a letter he wrote to one of his spiritual daughters, and **(ii)** from an excellent English biography of St. Pio written by Rev Charles Mortimer Carty.

(i)

A Letter from St. Padre Pio to Annita Rodote

Pietrelcina, July 25, 1915.

Volume III of Correspondence with his Spiritual Daughters

Our Lady of Grace Capuchin Friary,

San Giovanni Rotondo, Italy, 1994.

"In order to avoid irreverence and imperfections in the house of God, in church - which the divine Master calls the house of prayer - I exhort you in the Lord to practice the following.

Enter the church in silence and with great respect, considering yourself unworthy to appear before the Lord's Majesty. Amongst other pious considerations, remember that our soul is the temple of God and, as such, we must keep it pure and spotless before God and his angels. Let us blush for having given access to the devil and his snares many times (with his enticements to the world, his pomp, his calling to the flesh) by not being able to keep our hearts pure and our bodies chaste; for having allowed our enemies to insinuate themselves into our hearts, thus desecrating the temple of God which we became through holy Baptism.

Then take holy water and make the sign of the cross carefully and slowly.

As soon as you are before God in the Blessed Sacrament, devoutly genuflect. Once you have found your place, kneel down and render the tribute of your presence and devotion to Jesus in the Blessed Sacrament. Confide all your needs to him along with those of others. Speak to him with filial abandonment, give free rein to your heart and give him complete freedom to work in you as he thinks best.

When assisting at Holy Mass and the sacred functions, be very composed when standing up, kneeling down, and sitting, and carry out every religious act with the greatest devotion. Be modest in your glances; don't turn your head here and there to see who enters and leaves. Don't laugh, out of reverence for this holy place and also out of respect for those who are near you. Try not to speak to anybody, except when charity or strict necessity requests this.

If you pray with others, say the words of the prayer distinctly, observe the pauses well and never hurry.

In short, behave in such a way that all present are edified by it and, through you, are urged to glorify and love the heavenly Father.

On leaving the church, you should be recollected and calm. Firstly take your leave of Jesus in the Blessed Sacrament; ask his forgiveness for the shortcomings committed in his divine presence and do not leave him without asking for and having received his paternal blessing.

Once you are outside the church, be as every follower of the Nazarene should be. Above all, be extremely modest in everything, as this is the virtue which, more than any other, reveals the affections of the heart. Nothing represents an object more faithfully or clearly than a mirror. In the same way, nothing more widely represents the good or bad qualities of a soul than the greater or lesser regulation of the exterior, as when one appears more or less modest. You must be modest in speech, modest in laughter, modest in your bearing, modest in walking. All this must be practiced, not out of vanity in order to display one's self, nor out of hypocrisy in order to appear to be good to the eyes of others, but rather, for the internal virtue of modesty, which regulates the external workings of the body."

(ii)

Padre Pio The Stigmatist

by Rev Charles Mortimer Carty,

Clonmore and Reynolds Ltd. 1957. (p 30).

"It is not surprising that the name of Padre Pio has given rise to the most fantastic legends and completely spurious accounts of his life and deeds. He was credited with innumerable false prophecies, and unauthorised books and pamphlets have been circulated about him in Europe and the United States.

Here are some points to remember when hearing such assertions:

1. Fr Pio never makes prophecies concerning world events. He may predict something as the bombing of Genoa.
2. He never published or had others publish revelations.
3. When asked his opinion of visions and visionaries he always answers: 'This is not my affair. It is up to the Bishops, the Ecclesiastical authorities to decide such matters'.
4. When the Church has made a decision, as in the case of Heroldsbach (Germany) and Necedah, Wisconsin etc, Fr Pio when asked about these cases says very emphatically: 'People must obey their Bishops'.

5. Letters supposed to have been written by him after 1924 are automatically spurious, by the very fact that Fr Pio scrupulously and reverently obeys his superiors who have forbidden him to write since that year."

On that note this dedication can be concluded.

Quotations

Scripture

"Abraham took the wood for the burnt offering, and *laid it on Isaac his son*; and he took in his hand the fire and the knife. So they went both of them together. And Isaac said to his father Abraham, 'My father!' And he said, 'Here am I, my son.' He said, 'Behold, the fire and the wood; but where is the lamb' ... Abraham said, 'God will provide himself the lamb'..." (Gen 22: 6-7)

"The next day he saw Jesus coming toward him and declared, 'Here is the Lamb of God who takes away the sins of the world'!" (John 1: 29)

St Pio

"Every Holy Mass, heard with devotion, produces in our souls marvelous effects, abundant spiritual and material graces which we ourselves do not know."
"It is easier for the earth to exist without the sun than without the Holy Sacrifice of the Mass."

Fr John Hardon S.J.

"When Pope Urban IV (1261-1264) first established the Feast of Corpus Christi, he requested St. Thomas Aquinas (1225-1274) to compose hymns for it. Among the five beautiful hymns Aquinas composed in honor of Jesus in the Blessed Sacrament was the *Lauda Sion Salvatorem,* which is worth quoting at some length because it is such a treasure of our faith.

> 'Christ's followers know by faith that bread is changed into His flesh and wine into His blood. Man cannot understand this, cannot perceive it; but a lively faith affirms that the change, which is outside the natural course of things, takes place. Under the different species, which are now signs only and not their own reality, there lie hidden wonderful realities. His body is our food, His blood our drink. And yet Christ remains entire under each species. The communicant receives the complete Christ - uncut, unbroken, and undivided. Whether one receives or a thousand, the one receives as much as the

thousand. Nor is Christ diminished by being received. The good and the wicked alike receive Him, but with the unlike destiny of life or death. To the wicked it is death, but life to the good. See how different is the result, though each receives the same. Last of all, if the sacrament is broken, have no doubt. Remember there is as much in a fragment as in an unbroken host. There is no division of the reality, but only a breaking of the sign; nor does the breaking diminish the condition or size of the One hidden under the sign.'

In addition to *Lauda Sion Salvatorem*, St. Thomas wrote *Adoro Te Devote*, *Pange Lingua*, *Sacris Sollemnis* and *Verbum Supernum*. *Lauda Sion Salvatorem* is the Sequence before the Gospel on Corpus Christi. The last two verses comprise the well known Bone pastor, panis vere."

St. Francis of Assisi

"What wonderful majesty! What stupendous condescension! O sublime humility! That the Lord of the whole universe, God and the Son of God, should humble Himself like this under the form of a little bread, for our salvation."

St. Jerome

"If Christ did not want to dismiss the Jews without food in the desert for fear that they would collapse on the way, it was to teach us that it is dangerous to try to get to heaven without the Bread of Heaven."

St. John Chrysostom

"How many of you say: 'I should like to see His face, His garments, His shoes'. You do see Him, you touch Him, you eat Him. He gives Himself to you, not only that you may see Him, but also to be your food and nourishment."

"When the Mass is being celebrated, the sanctuary is filled with countless angels, who adore the Divine Victim immolated on the altar."

Pope St. Pius X

"The devotion to the Eucharist is the most noble, because it has God as its object; it is the most profitable for salvation, because it gives us the Author of Grace; it is the sweetest, because the Lord is Sweetness Itself."

St. Teresa of Avila

"Here on earth it's impossible to perform a more meritorious act than visiting Jesus often in the Eucharist. If you took all of the good works done by all of the humans who have ever lived in all of history and stacked them all up and multiplied them by a million, they wouldn't equal the merit, the virtue and the worth of one Mass. The Eucharistic sacrifice is Christ's infinite merit, infinite value."

Table of Contents

Prolegomena

That which should be read first

The worldwide scandal that Catholic children come out of Catholic schools with no knowledge whatsoever of the Catholic Church, of Her Catholic Truth, Her Dogmas, Her infallible Tradition *and Her uniqueness*, goes on unabated. A whole generation of Catholics has been lost, and everywhere anti-discriminatory legislation has been put in place which forbids the few Catholic parents who care from laying the blame at the doorstep of bishops, priests and religious. The great majority of Catholics are quite happy with the 'easy church' which the Modernists have erected as a substitute for the Catholic Church, and held up everywhere as the "modern Catholic Church", "the new Catholicism", given to the world, so they claim, by the Second Vatican Council. That this has resulted in darkness and absolute chaos in spiritual matters on a grand scale is understandable. The lifelong task of so many bishops of calculating and weighing how much Modernism they can filter into their dioceses against the God-given Light of the Magisterium and Tradition of the Catholic Church has been accurately foreseen and foretold.

> **"What has become of their Catholicity? Alas, this organisation** (SILLON, composed of well-meaning social Catholics in France) **which formerly afforded such promising expectations, has been harnessed in its course by the modern enemies of the Church, and is now no more than a miserable affluent, feeding** THE GREAT MOVEMENT OF APOSTASY, **being organised in every country for the establishment of a One-World Church, which shall have neither dogmas nor hierarchy neither discipline of the mind nor curb for the passions, and which, under the pretext of freedom and human dignity, would bring back to the world the reign of legalised cunning and brute force and of the oppression of the weak and of all those who toil and suffer...We know only too well the *dark* work-shops in which are elaborated those mischievous doctrines."**
>
> (*Our Apostolic Mandate*, Pope St. Pius X, 1910)

Many readers may feel that the word '*affluent*' in the above quote should read '*effluent*'.

The French of *Our Apostolic Mandate*, the language in which this Apostolic Letter was written and which I have in my possession, has '*affluent*', which is the correct word. The whole Modernist movement is *ad-fluent*, i.e. *flowing towards*, the great movement of apostasy. To stress that, I use the word 'feeding'. *Ex-fluent* is flowing out and that is weak here. The Pope and Saint was well aware that the Modernist movement was flowing out of the Church, but it was for him far more important to stress where it was flowing TO, Latin *ad*, and what it was feeding.

Flourishing worldwide Catholicism of barely forty years ago has been harnessed in its course by the modern enemies of the Church, the Modernists, who overnight have abandoned Her in droves. They are now no more than the miserable affluent the Pope and Saint spoke about in the above quote, feeding the great movement of apostasy organised in every country for the establishment of a One-World 'Church', *The World Council of Churches*, or WCC, which is anything but the Catholic Church.

And then this far-seeing Pope and Saint gave us in great detail the hallmarks by which this world-wide movement of apostasy can be recognised:

It will show itself as a '*religious monstrosity*' with **no Creed** (no dogma), with an **abandoned authority** (no Hierarchy), with **no Truth** (no discipline of the mind), and **with a total disregard for moral responsibility** (no curb on the passions). And who is there 'living' in today's world, who can say that all this has ***not*** come to pass, is ***not*** with us at this very moment in history and has ***not*** been fulfilled to the letter?

All this would be bad enough if it were all this Holy Father could have truthfully said about this great movement of apostasy. But he added much more to it. No doubt many observant students of the world scene could have guessed a hundred or so years ago, that a world unshackled from a Divinely revealed Creed, and freed from the guidance of a God-willed Authority, would end up as a world in which there would be no Truth, no longer any moral absolutes and therefore no curb on the passions. But to all this, this holy man from God added something that no one could have known beforehand unless lifted up by God and placed right in the middle of what would be going on in the very heart of life in the second half of the twentieth century. The Saint foretold that this modernistic 'counter-church', this religious monstrosity, this great movement of apostasy, **would use pretence.** And he gives us two examples of this pretence: the pretext of **freedom** and the pretext of **human dignity.** And since any pretence is not inspired by Truth, and so is Godless no matter how much the mass media would like us to believe otherwise, both these pretexts mentioned by Pope St. Pius X are part and parcel of this great apostasy.

But the present Holy Father *John Paul II* has added his voice to this global chorus of '*freedom*' and '*human dignity*', speaking so often about both these qualities but from the totally different panorama of Catholic Faith. To this the Modernists add their daily noisy reminder *ad nauseam* that our *human dignity* exists solely in our *total freedom* to do as we like. After all, aren't we all children of God? So how will we ever know in the darkness that surrounds us everywhere which are the freedom and human dignity that come from God and which are the false ones spread around by the world of the Beast, by all the Modernists and by the WCC?

With regard to this difficulty, Pope *St. Pius X* has not left us in any doubt in spite of the sickening darkness in which we have to find our way. For he has made it abundantly clear which freedom and human dignity come from God and which ones are used as a pretence by the great movement of apostasy. The *freedom* and *human dignity* preached by the Modernists, by the WCC and by all those who no longer believe in any dogma, who no longer accept a transcendental truth, who no longer obey a God-given authority and who no longer admit to the existence of an objective and absolute morality imposed on everyone, such *freedom* and *human dignity* are used as a *pretext* to do evil. They are, according to the Saint's own words, used for

- **the reign of legalised cunning,**
- **the use of brute force,** and so for
- **the oppression of the weak and of all those who toil and suffer….**

And I repeat that this astounding precision of the very essence of our time could never have come from guesswork but only from a direct revelation by God.

We only have to turn on the television, open a newspaper or a modern magazine anywhere in the world to see how literally the prophecy of Pope St. Pius X has been fulfilled. The push of the homosexual network, the strident demands of feminism, the harsh legislations of governments, the 'freedom' of big business by which the poor are oppressed and sucked dry to increase the wealth of the rich, the brute force by which minor offences against unjust laws are being punished whereas the rich offenders against just laws can buy for themselves exemptions: it all adds up to a world without fear of God, a world of no belief in Revealed Truths, of no hierarchical values, no discipline of the mind and no curb on the passions. In other words, a world of pretence and pretexts, a world of total license for those who can afford this "legalised cunning" for their own advantage, and of oppression for those who cannot.

All of this has been dealt with and explained in books and articles already written. And great consolation for the readers has been derived from the parallel drawn in these books and articles between the Sacred Passion of Our Blessed Lord and Saviour Jesus Christ and sustained by His Holy Mother on that first Good Friday 2000 years ago, and the Sacred Passion at present undergone by Our Lord's Mystical Body, our Holy Mother the Catholic Church, freely accepted on His behalf and example by the Second Vatican Council.

But next to a small minority of Catholics who, in the supernatural light of their untrammelled Catholic Faith are fully aware of what is going on, and who try to live according to that Light, are a great majority of Catholics who either left the Church altogether, or who no longer practise their Faith. And to this vast number must be added those who are critical of Vatican II and of the Popes who implemented its prescriptions, and are now truly uncomprehending and bewildered in the darkness that has overtaken us. For their closed minds the teachings of Vatican II and the above-quoted predictions of Pope St. Pius X are a closed book. Thus they will not apply to themselves the serious warnings contained in them as well as in the words of this Holy Pope we are going to quote now.

For, apart from the message already dealt with, this Pope and great Saint also wrote the following immortal words to be read by every Catholic on earth:

> "They (i.e. the Modernists) (*Pascendi*, 1907) lay the axe not to the branches and shoots, but to the very root, i.e. to the Faith and its deepest fibres. And once having struck at this Root of Immortality, they proceed to diffuse poison through the whole tree".

These momentous words do ***not*** reveal any damage to the Faith of the Catholic Church *as such* which of course is impossible, no matter to what low numbers the True Church may eventually be reduced on this planet. But they most certainly refer to an impairment of the Catholic Faith in millions of Catholics the world over.

<u>This poisoning of Catholic minds goes to the heart of the modern problem</u>.

Thus this book is written and published for the small minority of Catholic parents who want their children to be brought up in the timeless and eternal stream of Catholic Truth and practice as they are contained in, and learned from, the Catholic Mass. For as soon as the love for the Blessed Sacrament has struck its deep roots in the souls of their children, they know from their own experience and from the Lives of the Saints, that it will never leave them. For It truly is "*the treasure in the field*" (Mat. 13:44) and "*the pearl of great beauty*" (Mat. 13:46), for which the trader-in-the-know sold everything in order to possess it.

In dealing with this great Mystery of the Catholic Faith it is very necessary that it be done systematically. What happened at the Last Supper, when Christ, as the Pascal Lamb, changed bread into His Sacred Body, and wine into His most precious Blood, extended backwards in time all through the Old Testament right up to Adam and Eve, and was linked irrevocably to His atoning Death on the Cross the next day. Parents who want their children to have a good understanding of this, must take their time to make all the necessary connections.

The book will take care of this, but it will require of adults that they read up on it first in order to keep before their children and young adults *the grand total* from which the finer details must be explained. But they should have no fear in the exercise of this spiritual work of mercy, keeping before them the words spoken by Our Lord:

> "I bless You, Father, Lord of heaven and earth, for hiding these things from the learned and the clever, and revealing them to mere children. Yes, Father, for that is what it pleased You to do… No one knows the Father except the Son and those to whom the Son chooses to reveal Him" (John 11:25-26).

Thus the book has not been divided in chapters but in sections, all related to one another. The first section deals with the reason why the Son of God was sent by the Father to our earth. The rest follows from that.

Part I

The Catholic Mass

Section One

Preliminaries

The Fall of Eve

For the profound understanding of what the Blessed Trinity had in mind with the creation of Eve, it is not sufficient to understand that He created her *female,* that He created her as a *helpmate,* and that He created her for her future role as the *mother* of all the living. To understand how the Early Church grasped the role of Christ as the *New Adam* and the role of Mary and His Marian Church as the *New Eve,* it is important to realise that the Church saw Herself in an identical relationship to Christ as Eve was to Adam: <u>as the *Body* under Her Head</u>. This unbreakable bond had been established through the enduring espousal of a Bride to Her Groom in holy Matrimony. And since Our Lady is truly the beginning of the Church, then She too saw Herself, '*as the New Eve of the New Covenant*', in the same mystical union to Her Son as God had willed Eve in relation to Adam: *in the one, indivisible unity of body and head.* And it is only from this original union between body and head that all the other names of Eve and Our Lady: *female, helpmate* and *mother,* take their meaning. It is of the utmost importance that we keep clearly before the eyes of our minds that God never willed His Son on earth to act on His own, but, as St. Paul has stated so clearly, as the Head of a Body, His Mystical Body, the Catholic Church. And this Body, this Church, was always there, because Mary was the beginning of it. So the Head never acted in isolation from His Body, and Mary and the Holy Marian Church never acted in isolation from Her Head.

From this it follows that, right from the start, ever since His Mother gave Her consent to the Archangel Gabriel, Christ and Mary were not only irrevocably united as Son and Mother, but, for the sake of our Redemption, even more intimately as Head and Body. Christ, on the full strength of this unanimous teaching in the whole of the Catholic Church's Sacred Tradition, did not go through His Passion alone. His Body the Church was there suffering with Him in the person of the Blessed Virgin Mary, the beginning of that Church, accompanied by all the disciples who, as the members of that Church, underwent with Her all the sufferings of Christ the Head.

This doctrine of the Holy Church is so important that we do well to study its contrast. To study how Eve, in complete isolation from Adam her head, did her own thing and so fell from grace into mortal sin. This will be a great help for us to understand how Mary and the Church worked in union with Christ the Head to destroy the original sin of Adam and Eve and to restore to mankind its original state of Grace.

Our starting point thus is Eve, the object of intense scrutiny by Satan, in order that we may learn by contrast what God is going to reveal about the nature of His future Helpmate, an as yet Mystery Woman, 'the Woman of Genesis'. In much of what follows I acknowledge my indebtedness to the scholarship displayed by that astute and erudite exegete, G. H. *Pember*, MA, in his remarkable book of 1876, *Earth's Earliest Ages.* I pick up the paraphrasing of Pember's account where he says:

'We must now return to Adam and Eve whom we left enjoying in innocence the pleasures which

God had provided for them. But short indeed was their time of happiness, for the powers of evil were already setting the fatal snare, instigated no doubt at this stage to their foul purpose by pure malignity: to oppose God at every turn.

The course of action adopted by Satan shows that God had not deprived him of his powerful intellect, although it had been changed by his own fall from the noble power of a prince of the Most High to a base cunning of a deceitful intriguer. He would not make his assault with power and terror, for that would drive the assailed into the arms of their Protector instead of alluring them away from Him. He would present himself in the form of an inferior and subject animal, from which they would never suspect harm. For, like all his seed of this world, Satan, though proud even to destruction can yet degrade himself to the very dust in order to carry out his deadly purpose. Neither would he consider approaching the man and the woman together, for combined, they might uphold one another in their duty of obedience and love of God. And he well knew that, once he was detected, a second attempt would be met with far greater resistance. And finally, several reasons seem to have deterred him from tempting Adam alone. For one, had he begun by overcoming the man, and then through him worked the fall of the woman, her ruin would have been incomplete. She would not have been wholly without excuse before God since she would have acted on the orders or under the influence of the one *whom He had set over her as her head.* But a deeper, more subtle, and so a more cogent reason would have been that his study of the male and female natures and psychologies revealed to Satan the important differences in qualities and temperament with which a wise Creator had endowed each *to complement the other.* Having accurately grasped that in both natures the strongest qualities become the weak point when isolated, that is, when they are *not used for the perfection of the partner* but for the gratification of self, he must have come to the conclusion that, for the purpose of his devious scheme, the misdirection of the female qualities and endowments would meet with the greater chance of success.'

Here we may interrupt the quoting and paraphrasing of Pember's account of the lead-up to the

Fall, and point to the complete and savage disregard for the beautiful balance between the male and female qualities displayed by the 'feminists' of our days. For the destruction of this balance is pursued exclusively 'for the gratification of self', which is destroying the femininity in their followers. This degradation of both sexes is by now being finalised into law in many 'civilised' countries, as a weapon in the final onslaught on the only Church created in the image and likeness of a Virgin!

Influenced, then, by considerations such as these, we find Eve by herself in the vicinity of the 'tree of good and evil'. God's command had been clear, and was fully open for prayerful reflection and meditation, leading to a deeper understanding of God, and love for Him. It was also fully open to female curiosity and speculation! The first road would be taken by Eve's complete counterpart many centuries later: "*But Mary kept all these words, pondering them in her heart*" (Lk. 2:19, 51). In this She was acting in accordance with what Her holy forefather Jacob had done: *His brothers therefore envied him (Joseph), but the father considered this matter with himself* (Gen. 37:11). Maybe the beautiful addition found in St. Luke: "in her heart", was missing in Eve. Maybe she did not love God's command sufficiently yet; and so her speculations remained idle curiosity in her mind, without being allowed entry into her heart as a basis for prayer.

From the recorded conversation with the devil which now follows in Scripture, we may conclude that she was musing on the strangeness of God's prohibition near the fatal tree: 'Wherefore had He planted the tree in their garden if they were not to enjoy it? What so great difference could there be between it and the other trees, of which they could eat freely?' Maybe even a more strongly felt curiosity may have moved her to examine the forbidden object more closely in order to see if she could detect its peculiarity.

That Eve was here on a crossroad is obvious. Had she allowed these legitimate questions to enter into her heart where she could ponder them prayerfully with God, as was her duty and privilege as creature, she would have found all the correct answers.

As it was, when Eve was standing near the tree, her guard dangerously low, 'a serpent approached and addressed her'. That she was not at all startled by such an occurrence seems to point to the existence of an intelligent communication between man and the inferior creatures before the Fall. But we must not of course think of the serpent as the repulsive and venomous reptile to which we feel now an instinctive antipathy. For it had not been cursed, but held itself upright, one of the most intelligent, and probably the most beautiful, of all the beasts of the field. The creature was thus still free from (physical) venom, and not improbably winged, while its scales glittered in the sun's rays like deep-burnished gold. It must have been a most arresting sight. Little did Eve suspect that beneath that beautiful and apparently innocent form lurked a most powerful (and for her spiritual well being a most venomous) enemy.

"Can it be true that God has forbidden you to eat of any tree in the garden?"

So began Satan the opening up one of the most far-reaching conversations ever recorded in human history. Simple as this crafty question may seem at first appearance, it was full of dangerous guile, so marvellously adapted to the purpose of disturbing still further the moral fibre of the woman whose disquiet had begun with musings of the mind only, without being allowed entry into her heart for prayerful consideration with her God.

In preparing the way for one's complete subversion, the skilled tempter invariably uses openings afforded by the thoughts of those approached. Here we hear Eve's musings spoken out aloud by Satan, and we see him drive a wedge between the near perfection of Eve, as she had come forth from the hands of the Creator, and His all perfect creature she is yet to become. The tempter puts to her the sly suggestion that she abstains, because God has harshly forbidden her and her husband to touch any of all that delicious fruit around them. And so by this brief but most skilful question, Satan begins an interrogation which envelops his unsuspecting victim in the fog of potentially grave error, strongly insinuated to her from at least five suggestions.

1. First, he throws her off guard by his assumed ignorance.
2. Then, he stirs up vanity from the depth of her self-consciousness by giving her an op-

portunity to correct him and so remain 'in dialogue' with him.

3. Thirdly, he uses the term 'Elohim' for God and not the covenant name 'Yahweh', to present the Creator as remote and as having little concern with His creatures.
4. After that he puts a doubt in her mind as to whether God had really uttered the prohibition, thereby strongly suggesting the possibility of a mistake.
5. Lastly, he insinuates to her the blasphemous thought that harshness and caprice on God's part are not inconceivable but indeed may sometimes be expected.

Once again we may interrupt the lead-up to Eve's fall for two considerations.

In the first one of these I wish to draw the attention of the reader to the compelling accuracy and timelessness of God's Revelation in Sacred Scripture. How could the thoughts of those reading the above be prevented from straying away from the setting in the Garden of Eden to the uncanny similarity of our modern 'Eves', faced with the equally forbidden fruit of the 'contraceptive pill'? What harshness the sure command does assume, if it is only considered *in the mind,* without being allowed prayerful consideration with God *in the heart.* How remote and unconcerned God could become, if He is not seen as the Father who with His command is closer to us and our real happiness than we are to ourselves?

And what are we to make of all those bishops and priests who, like the serpent in the Garden, diminish the Divine command with disturbing appeals to loopholes or individual consciences? Are the innuendos of 'harshness' and even 'caprice' on the part of God all that far removed from the minds of such bishops and priests, and so-called theologians and catechists? Do we not detect here again as we did before, the terrible vengeance of God on all those who interfere with His Holy Tradition in the mistaken belief that Genesis chapters 1 - 11 are nothing but a collection of myths? Stories with no bearing on the 'Real reality' as it is known to 'modern man', that pathetic end-product of a faked evolution? Is not this whole affair covered by Divine Inerrancy affirming the reality of the devil's first question? Meant as an instruction for every woman after Eve, including all the modern women-on-the-pill? And as a dire warning for all those, who would like to assume the role of Satan in these matters, bringing doubt to Catholic minds?

The other matter I would like to draw attention to at this stage of the narrative is Pember's astute observation of the distinction between the two names for God in the Hebrew Bible: 'Elohim' and 'Yahweh'. One of the crumbling pillars of salt on which the tattered remains of the *Documentary Hypothesis* claims its so-called 'researches' to rest, is the totally unwarranted and equally unfounded fable that these different names for God must point to two different 'sources' for the writing of Genesis: one the so-called 'Elohist' document, the other 'Yahwist'. This was then accepted as 'proof' that Genesis was composed at a much later date, from which then the inevitable conclusion must be drawn that, unfortunately, Moses can no longer be considered to be the author of Genesis. For, so the argument goes, if he was, he would not have jumped from the use of one Name of God to the other.

Earlier in his book Pember has drawn attention to this reasoning. This means that already by 1876, when the rationalist onslaught on Holy Scripture in the form of the 'Higher Critique' (of which the *Documentary Hypothesis* of our days is the poisonous fruit) was in full swing, reasoned argument against it was well known.

Pember started off with the observation that there is no mention of a covenant of God with Adam in the first chapter of Genesis, for there we have primarily a record of creation, and the injunction to the man to dress and watch over the Garden. At that stage he needed nothing more, for knowing well the single prohibition of his God, he could at once detect a foe in any being tempting him to disobey it. Immediately after this, we have the detailed account, in the so-called 'Second Creation Story' of how God-Yahweh came into covenant with man. In this supplementary account we are concerned with the moral responsibility of man. And immediately we are met with a change in the appellation of God. When looked upon only as Creator and Ruler, He is referred to as Elohim: God, the Mighty One. But as soon as He appears in covenant relation with man,

He takes the title of Yahweh: God, the Lord. At its very first introduction the Name Yahweh is joined with Elohim to obviate any doubt as to the identity of the One Being, designated by both names, even when used separately.

"Now it is evident" continues Pember "that while either of these names is likely to suit some passages, there must nevertheless be many cases in which the one would be more appropriate than the other. Of this the sacred writers are always mindful and we will presently meet with other instances of their careful discrimination. It thus appears that the occurrence of the two Names of God, adduced by the Rationalists as a proof that the Scriptures are a clumsy compilation of diverse and incongruous documents to which they give the names 'Elohistic' and 'Yahwistic' as to two imaginary 'sources', that this occurrence far from demonstrating the validity of their argument, shows the very opposite and beautifully exhibits the unity and consistency of the whole volume".

With our friend Pember and all the other scholars who have no use for the 'Documentary Hypothesis' we may attach great significance to the fact that

Adam carefully records, that Satan used the word *Elohim* as God's Name when addressing a woman he knew to be in holy covenant with God and so knew Him much more intimately as her Lord *Yahweh.* The significance of this digression will come to light immediately.

Returning now to the analysis of the temptation of Eve in the garden, we see from her answer the blinding effect this first question of the devil had on her.

She states that they could eat of the other trees in the garden, and had only been warned away from the one in the centre. Of this one alone "God had commanded us that we should not eat of it, and that we should not touch it, lest perhaps we die" (Douay translation). But God had not prohibited them to touch it! Thus we may read in the exaggeration of this added clause a secret discontent as well as an inclination to set the command of the Almighty, 'God-Elohim', in as harsh a light as possible.

Nor is this all; not only does Eve increase the stringency of the law, she also weakens the penalty. God had declared: "Thou shalt surely die", which she alters to "lest perhaps we die" (Gen. 3:3, Douay version).

Doubt is already doing its work in her mind; she is now prepared to hear the Truth of God openly denied. It is clear from her inexcusable exaggeration of the Divine Imposition, that she had taken up Satan's lead into the dark, and speaks of her Creator and Benefactor as *Elohim*, the 'Power', mighty indeed, but to men vague, distant, and almost unknown. For the success of his advances, Satan had recognised the necessity to banish from her heart all thought of a near and closely connected God, and she accepts his suggestion and co-operates with him. For the image of *Yahweh* and His Sacred Covenant are rapidly fading from her mind and instead, self and sin are beginning to take its place.

Solemn indeed is the warning to her descendants when Eve's thoughts are analysed as revealed by her words, a warning to an offspring, by whose feet her own sad path is ceaselessly trodden. How often, when we are perfectly aware of some direct command of God which we do not wish to obey, are we seduced into an exaggeration of its magnitude until at length, by the continual play of evil imaginings, we almost arrive at its impossibility. At the same time, is there not an equal determination afoot today to diminish the importance of the Divine Commandments and also of the penalty, hell, bound to our transgressions not only by an Almighty and faraway God-Elohim, living beyond our earthly sphere "in inaccessible Light" (1 Tim. 6:16), but by a loving Father who cares for us more than we can ever love ourselves?

Satan quickly perceived the state of Eve's mind. His plan of attack was succeeding: she had begun to doubt! He instantly pressed his advantage by a bold lie "Ye shall not surely die"! Thus "the liar from the beginning" (Jo. 8:44) dared to place his own assertion in direct opposition to that of the Almighty. And Eve believed him, believed this beast of the field rather than God, as millions of Catholics now prefer to believe the innumerable contradictions and distortions of Catholic Dogma, disseminated by the Modernists on the say-so of a Teilhard de Chardin and his horde of Modernist 'theologians'.

"For God knows" pursued the tempter, "that in the day ye eat thereof; your eyes shall be opened and ye shall be as God, knowing good and evil".

On hearing this distortion of the Truth, Eve immediately knew two things:

(i) She did not know 'evil', and she was fully aware that she did not know it,
(ii) She <u>did</u> know that, whatever 'evil' was, she would never know it "as God knows".

At this desperately late hour it should have occurred to Eve that God also knew more: that this "opening of their eyes" would be no addition to their happiness but instead harmful and destructive. Otherwise, she could have reasoned, He would surely have given to them this 'higher knowledge' if it had been necessary for their happiness. Could she not by a moment's reflection perceive the fearful responsibility which the knowledge of this mysterious, unknown thing would necessarily involve, and bless the Lord God, Who had spared her from its perils? Or could she not at least trust the Love of Him Who had called her into being, and turn with horror and disgust from the blasphemous impiety which suggested to her the real possibility of in any way raising herself to His height? She could not for she was deceived, as St. Paul so clearly teaches in 1 Tim. 2:14: "Adam was not deceived, but the woman was deceived, and so became a transgressor". Her reason had become perverted by desire, a vision of self exaltation had intoxicated her. There had been no error in Satan's judgment: he had detected the weakest point when he appealed to her vanity and suggested to her the source of his own downfall: *the idea of becoming as God....*

And so Eve sinned ....

"The woman was deceived" said St. Paul "and so became a transgressor". Her deception and her terrible Sin were only in her mind! There were as yet no inordinate and rebellious passions in her. She did not fall through weakness, as we so often do. The direction which her thoughts took could, at any stage of the Temptation, have been scrutinised by her clear and objective mind and its mighty reasoning powers. But her uneasiness lay with the Divine Prohibition, which became unchecked when she deliberately withheld from it the power of prayer and the incisiveness of her as yet uncorrupted mind, and on which the devil seized to enlarge it to resentment, caused her to lapse into one of the worst possible states into which a soul can sink in the sight of God: unchecked and paralysing doubt! I say paralysing advisedly because it prevented her from taking refuge in prayer, when she deliberately refused to check with her Creator with whom she was in covenant, the devil's preposterous logic and claims.

Does the unprecedented paralysis of many bishops in the face of the preposterous 'logic' and claims of the Modernists and Teilhardians with regard to Catholic Truth show us that in our days too a grave doubt is present in episcopal minds; a doubt to which once again ready access to the powerful light of objective reasoning and scrutiny is being refused? Will prayer prove a substitute for this unwillingness if prayer demands an honest reappraisal and about-face? Could that be the reason why public devotion to the Mother of God is at an all-time low because 'the Woman of Genesis' is such a stark antithesis of this universal re-enactment of Eve's Sin?

The Downfall of Adam

After Eve's Sin, Adam's hands were tied: 'the knot of Eve'. (Vatican II, *Lumen Gentium*, #56).

Hard as it may be, it will nevertheless be very instructive for us to get some idea of what must have gone on in his mind, as yet unaffected by Sin.

Here was his wife, his helpmate, with the forbidden fruit in her hand, bent on his downfall. For, from the missing piece in the fruit, he realised with utter disbelief what must have happened. Giving in to her, he could clearly see, would constitute a transgression of the known Will of God, which would be anything but the right way to go about to come to the aid of his stricken wife. In fact, it would complicate matters no end. He could also see that nothing would be gained by reproaching her. The terrible deed had been irrevocably done.

In groping for a response he marked time by questioning her about the lead-up to her sorry state. But after having heard her out no additional light had been gained. The hard question remained: *What was he to do?*

In theory, three courses of actions were open to him:

1. He could refuse to eat from the forbidden fruit as was his duty as creature.

2. He could accept the fruit and eat it in the mistaken belief that accommodating his wife in this way would be the best way out.
3. He could turn to God in prayer for strength and enlightenment.

"*....in the mistaken belief....*

Since we must accept that St. Paul was inspired by the Holy Spirit when he wrote that "*Adam was not deceived*", in 1 Tim. 2:14, we must take this to mean that Adam was unable to claim *a mistaken belief* that eating from the fruit would be the best way out to come to the aid of his wife. He was fully aware that giving in to his wife in her dreadful shame and defeat was ***not*** the way to rectify matters. That left him with only two courses of action, (1) and (3) above.

This leads us to the deepest mystery of them all in that for mankind so crucial day: *why did Adam refuse to pray?* His refusal to pray shows that he had made up his mind to accommodate the creature, his wife, in preference to God. But *why* did he not turn to Yahweh his God with Whom he knew himself to be in covenant, if refusing to eat (1 above) appeared to him so very hard?

There can only be one answer that lies at the root of this refusal: ***doubt.*** As had been the case with his wife Eve: *a paralysing doubt.* Deep in his mind he had started to doubt if God really loved them. If God really cared for them. A nagging relief to take the easy way out by pretending that their Protector had abandoned them in not shielding his wife Eve from this terrible temptation.

How can we be so sure that it was only pretence that made Adam think like that? Because of what St. Paul wrote down some 4000 thousand years later:

"*Adam was not deceived*". And how could St. Paul be so sure? Because it is an Apostolic Tradition in the Holy Catholic Church, which means that it is a Tradition that has come down to us from the Apostles, that our first parents Adam and Eve were created in the state of Grace, that is, in Sanctifying Grace, the same state which is restored to us after the healing waters of Baptism, and which contains the three infused virtues of Faith, Hope and Love. Only by a deliberate act could these divine virtues be obscured and – as was the case here – be subsequently rejected.

His was a deliberate choice, a Sin of unprecedented malice in the human race: **'the Original Sin'.** For Adam knew that giving in to her was *not* the way to come to her aid and help her out of her disgrace as it entailed a previous rejection of God first. The helpmate had acted in total separation and alienation from her head; he willingly let her tie his hands and the result has been utter chaos..... For it is this state of enmity with God with its dire consequences that has been passed on to the entire human race from its very beginning with only one exception: the Immaculate Conception of the Blessed Virgin Mary.

Yes indeed, their eyes had been opened and now they knew good from evil. But, we may well ask, at what cost? And for what purpose?

And when God called, the One Who had created them with so much love *in His own image and likeness,* and Who, for that very purpose, had endowed them with the most stupendous gifts, natural as well as supernatural, they hid in their state of utter misery and shame....

The first recorded curse of God, the one pronounced against Satan after the temptation and fall of Adam and Eve, is exceedingly important as the punishment meted out there *involves human beings*:-

"And the Lord God said to the serpent,

'Because you have done this, be accursed beyond all cattle, all wild beasts. You shall crawl on your belly and eat dust every day of your life. I will make you enemies of each other, you and the Woman, your seed and Her Seed. She shall crush your head and you will strike at Her heel'." (Gen. 3:14-15.)

"Because you have done this...."

"There is to be no mistake as to the reason for the curse", writes Pember in his already quoted book: *Earth's Earliest Ages*. "It is no accident but the deeply-burnt brand which testifies to God's abhorrence of him who brought Sin into Creation."

What awesome thoughts for our contemporaries. How often, in human history, have bishops, priests, teachers and parents repeated the first apostasy? Enforced heresy on those entrusted to their care? Made Catholics believe them, and made them doubt the Voice of God as it became known to humanity in the teachings of the Catholic Church? How often has innocent Catholic Faith been extinguished by those occupying places of trust? Has the curse been mitigated so that they got away with it? Has History truly nothing to say about what is rampant in our days? Is it silent about the vengeance of God over the wilful extinction of Catholic Faith?

No, History has been far from silent! It has told us again and again: 'There will be no mistake! God's pronouncement to Satan is indeed a deeply-burnt brand'.

No matter how encouraging the popularity of a 'renewed catholicism' is to those who enforce it or allow it unhindered proliferation, it will turn out to be mere dust, coming from those condemned to live in dark places. The 'easy catholicism' of our times with its widespread use of 'general absolution', the revolt against '*Humanae Vitae*' with its widespread use of the contraceptive pill, the Modernism that teaches the absolute freedom of conscience to do one's own thing, programs like RENEW, the clamour for 'women priests' and for married priests, the formation of 'deaneries' for the smooth transition of all the benefits of the anti-hierarchical and anti-Genesis '*church of darkness*' into the renewed 'local churches': it will all prove to be dust, condemned to be empty of any real value, of human satisfaction or of lasting joy....

So, when God turned to Satan after the Fall, there was no hope of any relief for that stricken creature. But when He subsequently turned to Adam and Eve, it became a different story, a story indeed of punishment but mingled with Supernatural Hope.

Satan had deluded Eve into an alliance with himself against the Creator; but God would break up the confederation. The Covenant with Death would be annulled, the agreement with Hell would not stand forever. "I will put enmity between thee and the Woman" were His almighty words to the abashed and speechless serpent. Nor was it difficult for Satan to divine the meaning of this separation: he was cast out to perdition, but Eve the Lord would save in a New Covenant and with the direct intervention of the Seed of a future Woman, as yet unnamed.

Thus, in His loving kindness, God devised a plan of first pronouncing judgement on the serpent, thereby implying that the fallen should not sink hopelessly to the condition of their deceiver, but be set in sharp opposition to him. With the result that a bright ray of Hope broke in through their despair, giving them strength to hear pronounced to them their share of the punishment. And Adam understood as far as that was possible the promise by God of a future Redeemer. He put his faith in God, and by that simple act of surrender was prevented any alienation between himself and his wife Eve. "*And Adam called his wife 'Eve', the mother of all the living*" [Gen. 3:20].

After Adam had made his Profession of Faith in God, we immediately find the Lord returning to the mourners and rewarding their trust in His Promise by a further act of kindness and an extension of their knowledge. He took away their miserable coverings of fig leaves and clothed them with clothes of skins. By this simple act the Lord God testified to several things. First of all that their shame was not groundless, but that indeed there was need of a covering. Secondly he made clear that the best the sinners could do for themselves was of no avail. And beyond this they must learn that only by life can life be redeemed; that, if the sinner die not, there must be a Substitute, and that the Most High is Holiness and Justice as well as Love.

From these revelations in Genesis we learn that sacrifice by means of expiation must have been ordained by God Himself. Man could never have thought of such a thing, or have dared, in his worship, to take the life of one of God's innocent creatures, unless he had been commanded to do so. We may think it very likely then, that it was at this most appropriate moment that the Lord instituted the *rite of expiation* as a type of the Great Sacrifice to come. The sinful pair could not have been covered with the skins of sheep unless the animals had first been slaughtered. Just as the whole human race could never have been dressed to enter Heaven unless recreated by the infinite merits gained for it by the Death on the Cross of the Lamb of God.

Thus God killed the victims, and as He shed their life-blood, Adam and Eve for the first time gazed upon death with frightened eyes. Then He showed them how to lay the carcasses on the altar, that they might be an offering made by fire unto the Lord. Finally, He took the skins of the slain beasts and made of them the coats with which He clothed the trembling pair.

Thus the Gospel was preached from the beginning. "*The Lamb of God slain from the foundations of the world*" (Rev. 13:8), was revealed as soon as Sin had made His Death necessary.

The Victimhood of the Son of God

As has been explained in the foregoing, it is against the backdrop of the Fall of our first parents Adam and Eve, that God's promise in the Garden of Eden of a future Redeemer was made to the whole of mankind and is to be understood by us in that unbreakable link. It is contained in the words of condemnation He spoke to Satan.

We Catholics know that this future Woman, *the Woman of Genesis*, is the Blessed Virgin Mary, and that Her Seed, Her Son, born from Her virginity, is God the Son, the Son of the Eternal Father, the second Person of the Blessed Trinity, the Word of God made Man.

The Victimhood of God....

Where did it come from? When did it take its beginning? When did it culminate at its highest point? And how was it passed on to His very own Church? The answer to each of these questions is vital for on them is depended the supply of lifeblood for a Church founded to stand in for sinners; founded to be a victim!

St. John tells us when it started: "*....the Lamb which was slain from the foundation of the world*." (Rev. 13:8). This means the Victimhood of the future Redeemer became manifest as in a sign when the first sacrificial lambs were slain to dress the delinquent pair of our first parents after the Promise. (Gen. 3:21). But at that time there was not the slightest inkling that this future Redeemer of the whole of mankind would be the Son of God Himself, "*God from God*", as we say in the Sunday Creed.

St. Paul tells us where the decision was taken: "*according to the revelation of the Mystery which was kept secret from Eternity*". (Rom. 16:25).

Here St. Paul reveals in his letter to the Romans why no one could fully know the identity of the future Redeemer before the Son of God, Our Lord and

Saviour Jesus Christ, had come on earth, to make known completely the Mind of the Father as well as the purpose of the Holy Church He Himself was in the process of founding to complete His work after He had gone back to the Father.

The answer to the third question above *Where did it culminate? What was its high point?* Must be answered with St. Paul:- *At the Last Supper, Holy Thursday, sustained until 3 p.m. the next day!*

> "This is what I received from the Lord and in turn have passed on to you: that on the same night He was betrayed, the Lord Jesus took some bread, thanked God for it, broke it and said, 'This is My Body which is handed over for you; do this as a memorial of Me'. In the same way He took the cup after supper and said: 'This Cup is the New Covenant in My Blood. Whenever you drink it, do this as a memorial of Me'. Until the Lord comes, therefore, every time you eat this Bread and drink this Cup, you are proclaiming His Death". [1 Cor. 11:23-27]. (2nd Reading on Holy Thursday).

Where else do the poverty and privations the Son of God embraced here on earth for our salvation, His sufferings and humility, His obedience and Love, His meekness in rejection, and finally His strength in His Passion, and the power of His atoning Death on the Cross, all come together but in the Most Blessed Eucharist? Where else do we find the source and the symbol of all Victimhood and forgiveness until the end of time? How else could He show us the *natural lifestyle* of His Mystical Body the Church, perpetuated until the end of time in His very own Victim Souls.

The decision at the Last Supper to change bread and wine into His own Body and Blood may defy logic! Yet after enjoying its Fruits for two thousand years the Holy Church still exclaims with perfect rationale: "O Felix Culpa!" "Oh Happy Guilt to deserve such a Redeemer!" (Easter Saturday). It is from the very Foundations of Christianity that the Holy Church has always believed and taught as Catholic Dogma that Our Lord in His first Consecration at the Last Supper, really offered Himself as a sacrifice. The **mystical separation** of His Body and Blood: "*Here, this is My Body*", and "*Here, this* *is the Cup containing My Blood*", would not constitute a sacrifice, unless it was followed by a **real separation**, which took place that same night in His agony in the Garden of Olives and was sustained all the way right up to His death on the cross.

That way Christ became the real Pascal Lamb, which first had to be slain before His Body could be eaten, and His Blood could be drunk.

The Institution of the Blessed Eucharist was His Signature under His own death warrant, directly linking the prefigured separation of His Body and Blood at the Last Supper to the actual separation on Calvary within twenty four hours. And that Signature was written in Blood, "*blotting out the handwriting of the Decree that was against us*", (Col. 2:14). Thus, at the Last Supper, He fulfilled the Pascal Law and as the <u>sacrificed</u> Lamb of God He could give Himself as the Food from Heaven to His loved ones on their road from the slavery of Sin to their eternal Promised Land. It was *this sacrifice* at the Last Supper, linking every subsequent Consecration in any Catholic Mass to His atoning Death on Calvary, which He wanted perpetuated in His memory.

At the Incarnation Christ entered into the Sanctuary of His Mother's sacred womb, taking with Him His own Blood. And from then on every other sanctuary: the Cenacle, Golgotha, a Catholic Church or a soul in state of Sanctifying Grace, is modelled on that very first one, the one He loved most and was completely free to choose: the womb of His Mother, the Blessed Virgin Mary. From that moment on every genuine Sanctuary became a Marian Shrine, for it is true that Christ has written the Name of His Mother on the pillars of every Sanctuary He dwells in:

> "Those who prove victorious I will make into pillars in the Sanctuary of My God and they will stay there forever. I will inscribe on them the Name of My God, <u>and the Name of the City of My God</u>: the New Jerusalem and My own Name as well." (Rev. 3:12).

For nearly 2000 years the Blessed Virgin Mary has been revered by the faithful as "*the City of God*" It should not surprise us that there is only one Sanctuary, for there really is only one Sacrifice: "*Christ offered Himself only once*" (Heb. 9:28), and "*through the Blood of Jesus we have the right to enter the Sanctuary*" (Hebr. 10:19) to offer ourselves "to Him, with Him and in Him". *Every Catholic Mass is most truly the complete re-enactment of the great Sacrifice of Calvary.* On Calvary, Christ offered Himself *and his Church*, for He offered Himself as a Head: a Head of a Body, a Head <u>with</u> a Body. So perfect were Mary's cooperation and understanding at that most solemn moment, that She, by sacrificing Herself, completed the very way in which Christ wished to sacrifice Himself: as the head of His Church. In this way She acted as His most perfect Body, representing the whole Church, all of us, as the Mystical Body of Christ. Only in that way could that great, combined Sacrifice of our Head and His Body take place.

Christ's merits are unique and infinite, and they are His alone. But they are His "as flowing from the Head into His Body". But, and this is the Great Mystery of which St. Paul speaks: these merits were not earned in isolation. From all eternity it was apparently decreed by the Father that, with the infinite merits of His Son, there should be combined the finite contributions of the members of His Son's Body, to become the One, Great, Everlasting and Unbreakable Sacrifice of all times. So important is this Truth for the whole Church that God wished it to be made into the foundation of a Dogma, of the latest Marian Dogma: Mary's Assumption into Heaven. For it is this Truth, of the necessity of Mary's cooperation and contribution, revealed in Revelation and contained in Sacred Scripture, which enabled Pope Pius XII to trace the roots of Mary's Assumption to the sources of Revelation.

If this is the whole, revealed Truth about Christ's Sacrifice on Calvary, it is the whole, Dogmatic Truth of the re-enactment of that Sacrifice in every Catholic Mass. There the Priest, the faithful, in fact the whole Church, offer themselves in a real sense with Christ, the Victim of Calvary, and with Mary, His New Eve. In this way, in every age, the faithful people of God <u>can now do in person</u> what Mary did for them as their representative, completing in their own bodies, yet *as* His Body, what needed completing in the Passion of Christ, the Head.

Since the secret of holiness lies in the greatest possible union with God, the secret of sanctity here on earth must then lie in the greatest possible union with the Sacramental Christ. This then is the sole preoccupation of Our Blessed Lady and the secret of all Marian devotion. For truly Marian Catholics are made into truly Eucharistic Catholics. In the Blessed Eucharist we have the two great Truths of our Catholic religion combined: union with God and union with the Cross. So it is there that we find the Mother of the Lamb of God most active, and that is where we find the Bride, the children of the Mother, most closely united to Her. If the secret of the greatest sanctity lies in the Catholic Mass, then it can be no secret at all that the greatest evil, the ultimate in "the War on the Saints", must lie in the abolition of the Perpetual Sacrifice. We can point to a sure sign that the world is approaching the dreaded hour of this universal calamity: the ruthless campaign of terror and intimidation which Modernism is waging against "*all who hold and teach the Catholic Faith that comes to us from the Apostles*". The genuine Catholic love for the Two Victims whom God had joined together began to disintegrate in the public life of so-called "catholic communities" as well as in the private lives of many "modern Catholics": bishops, priests, religious, catechists, teachers, parents and children alike. I am of course referring here to the very Catholic love for the Blessed Sacrament and for the Blessed Virgin Mary. With this double-barrelled attack on the most precious possessions of the Holy Catholic Church, Modernism has dug its own grave. It is doomed. For these attacks had as their most unexpected result that worldwide Marian Catholics flocked to daily Mass where, as we saw, they become Eucharistic Catholics: those who learn how to be Victims! And Victimhood is still the most powerful state on earth!

We may finish these three preliminary sections in preparation of a treatise on the Catholic Mass with a prayer the Holy Church says on every Holy Thursday as Her '*Prayer over the Gifts*':

> **Lord, make us worthy to celebrate these Mysteries. Each time we offer this memorial Sacrifice** (i.e. the Holy Sacrifice of the Mass), **the work of our Redemption is accomplished.**

If every child in a Catholic school was taught these fundamental Truths leading them to a lifelong understanding of, and love for, the Holy Catholic Mass, the vast majority would never shirk their duty of attending Mass on every Sunday of the year.

Section Two

The Preparation

The Penitential Rite

As has become clear from what has been said so far, the Holy Sacrifice of the Mass is a repetition, or re-enactment, of what Christ Our Lord did at the Last Supper and what He subsequently did on Calvary. At the Last Supper Christ in an advanced, but not yet in a real way, separated for us His Body and His Blood. On Calvary the next day this separation did become the reality He foresaw and needed, in order that the repetition in time of these two great events could become "for us and for our salvation" the Holy Sacrifice of the Mass. This was done so that the Holy People in the Cenacle and on Calvary would not have a great advantage over us. If they were present at Christ's immolation of Himself, so can we be in the re-enactment of it. If they were able to offer themselves up with Him, so has it now been made possible for us to do the same.

The American Priest, *Fr. William Most*, has written some very beautiful things about this. This is what he said:

> "The Vatican Council says in No. 10 in her Constitution **'On the Sacred Liturgy'** that the Mass is the renewal of the new Covenant. Now in the renewal, (the Catholic Mass) there is, all readily admit, a twofold offering: the offering of Christ the Head to which is joined the offering of His members, which we are. We really do join with Him in the offering of the Mass.
>
> So then, if the **Renewal** is twofold, formed of the obedience of Christ to which is added that of His members, then would it not be strange if the **Original**, which the renewal repeats, did not have a similar twofold structure? Really, if the renewal were twofold and the original not, then the renewal would be partly false; it would not repeat fully what it should repeat.
>
> Therefore the original must have been twofold: Mary's offering, Her obedience, must have fused with the obedient offering of Christ. His obedience was the price of our Redemption. Her

obedience, says Vatican II, was joined with His. What else should that mean if not that She shared in paying the very price of that Redemption?"

(From *Vatican II - Marian Council*, pp. 26-27).

And we may ask again: "*What else would that mean if not that we too, as Her children, have our share in paying the very price of that Redemption*, if we attend with devotion the renewal of Calvary, the Catholic Mass?"

No wonder, then, that the serious business of this re-enactment of Calvary done by the whole Church whenever a Catholic Mass is being offered to God, is started with a suitable preparation, the Penitential Rite. For we cannot expect that we can fully partake in the offering up of this Holy Sacrifice if we do not make known to God and to each other how sorry we are for our own sins. For it is the forgiveness and expiation of sin which is the very reason for the Sacrifice on Calvary and for its renewal here in this church. And sins are not forgiven unless they are confessed with heartfelt sorrow.

"I confess to Almighty God,
And to you, here present,
That I have sinned through my own fault,
In my thoughts and in my words,
In what I have done, and in what I have failed to do.
And I ask Blessed Mary, ever Virgin,
And all the Angels and Saints,
And you here present,
To pray for me to the Lord our God".

The Gloria in Excelsis Deo

The Gloria is said or sung on all the great feast days of the Church and on most Sundays of the year except on the Sundays in Advent and Lent. Advent is the four-week preparation for the feast of Christmas, the Birth of Our Lord, and Lent is the six-week preparation for the feast of Easter, the Resurrection of the Lord. The "Glory to God in the highest", the literal translation of the above-quoted Latin text, was first sung to the shepherds in the fields around Bethlehem on the occasion of the birth of Our Lord in the stable. It expresses the joy of the whole Church over the fact that God has sent His only-begotten Son into the world to be our Redeemer from all sin and from all the effects of sin, including Death.

Glory to God in the highest,
And peace to His people on earth.
Lord God, heavenly King,
Almighty God and father,
We worship You, we give You thanks,
We praise You for your glory.
Lord Jesus Christ, only Son of the Father.
Lord God, Lamb of God,
You take away the sin of the world,
Have mercy on us.
You are seated at the right hand of the Father,
Receive our prayer.
For You alone are the Holy One,
You alone are the Lord,
You alone are the Most High,
Jesus Christ,
With the Holy Spirit,
In the glory of God the Father.
Amen.

After this expression of our thanks for God's forgiveness in the Penitential Rite, we can now turn to the Father to ask with great confidence to assist us in our need in the opening prayer of the Mass of the day.

After that we sit down to be instructed by God's Word in the Readings.

The Readings of the Day or for any Special Occasion

We all know how Christ has really never left us. He is still bodily present with us in the tabernacle of any Catholic church. This presence goes by the name 'the Blessed Sacrament' or 'the Blessed Eucharist'. But the Second Vatican Council saw fit to lay stress on another presence of Our Lord amongst us: His presence in the readings which follow the opening prayer. This presence is aptly called *the Liturgy of the Word.* And here we come across a very striking thing: the more we go to Mass during the week, the more we will find how apt these readings are for the situation in which we find ourselves during that day. Two people in entirely different circumstances hear the same readings, but draw from it exactly what the Holy Spirit wants them to hear. These readings truly are the Word of God, and the Word of God is infinite and limitless. It always provides for our immediate needs.

This should not really come as a surprise. From the time of the Apostles the Holy Church has taught that, before Christ became man and was born of the Virgin Mary on Christmas Day, He was the Son of God the Father, called by St. John '*the Word of God*' that is the total expression of the mind of God and the thoughts of His Father.

So, if the Son, the Word of God, is capable of expressing fully the infinite thoughts of God, He is capable of expressing for us from Sacred Scripture the thoughts of God for any human situation.

And thus we sit down and listen very attentively to the Word of God, a presence of God in our lives that is meant to help us through the day. In the most literal meaning of the word: *food* for thought….

The readings are taken from the Bible, the infallible and inspired Word of God.

Now the Holy Bible consists of two main parts: the Books of the Old Testament and the Books of the New Testament. The books of the Old Testament, (OT) were written before the coming of Christ on earth, and the Books of the New Testament (NT) were written after He had made His appearance as a Man amongst us. Since 'Testament' is another word for 'Covenant', we may say that the Books of the Old Testament relate the history of the Jewish people under the Old Covenant God had made with Abraham and later renewed and much extended under Moses. The New Covenant was, as is well-known, established in the Blood of Christ, in which the Baptism of the New Covenant replaces the circumcision of the Old.

The New Testament itself also consists of two very distinct parts: the four books that deal with the Life of Christ, called the four Gospels, and the rest of the books. The authors of the four Gospels are St. Matthew, St. Mark, St. Luke and St. John. As can be seen, only two of these, Matthew and John, were Apostles. St. Mark was not one of the Twelve, but was, what the Gospels call, a disciple. St. Luke was a convert, accepted into the Church by St. Paul. The remainder of the New Testament consists for the greater part of Letters, and also of The Acts of the Apostles, and the Book of Revelation by St. John. Fourteen of the Letters were written by St. Paul, two were written by St. Peter, the first Pope chosen by Christ Himself. Three were written by St. John. Of the remaining two Letters one was written by St. James, not the Apostle but a James who was known as 'the brother of Jesus', one of the Lord's many cousins, and the other by St. Jude, one of the Twelve Apostles. The 'Acts of the Apostles' was written by St. Luke.

All in all, the Books of the New Testament come to twenty-seven.

Since the Second Vatican Council, the readings for the Sunday Masses follow a three-year cycle, Year A, Year B and Year C. The readings for the daily Masses follow a two-year cycle, Year I and Year II. This was done so that most of the books of the Old and New Testament had a chance to put their rich content before the People of God.

Of the two, and sometimes three, readings, the last one, i.e. the Gospel reading, is always said by the Priest.

The first and second reading are divided by a "Responsorial Psalm", which, as the name indicates, is taken from part of one of the one hundred and fifty Psalms, which together make up one of the Books of the Old Testament. They have a bearing on the first reading.

For the sake of these readings and for the impact they have on the daily life of the faithful, it is important that, whilst they are read, they are followed from a missal.

The Homily

After the reading of the Gospel, those attending Mass sit down once again to listen to the *homily*, a short sermon on the readings, which is obligatory in a Sunday Mass, but optional for weekday Masses. But since the faithful are entirely at the mercy of the officiating Priest, and are dependent on how much he is in union with the Holy Spirit, not much can be said about homilies in this little booklet. The one thing that can truthfully be said about most homilies is, that they do not go to the root of Catholicism. They are so anaemic as to leave the hearers unmoved and comfortably *in their sins.* In other words, they are of a generic 'christianity' in line with all the Protestant sermons. Since in the great majority of cases nothing *specifically* Catholic is ever touched upon, they have become one of the most important preparations for the One-World 'Church', which according to the description Pope St. Pius X gave of this 'church' makes it anything but Catholic. The meagre food that most homilies dole out to robust Catholics would leave them spiritually starved had it not been for other arrangements which God has made for His most faithful servants: their deep insights into the Catholic Faith.

As an instance of this deplorable state of affairs, we may point here to the almost universal habit of instant canonisation of the dead in the 'homilies' of funeral Masses.

The Creed and the Prayers of the Faithful

The Sunday Creed is too important a prayer to be rushed through. So, in order to give Catholic parents and their children a chance to reflect on the all-important Articles of the Christian Faith it contains, it is printed here in full for private meditation.

I believe in one God, the Father the Almighty,
Creator of heaven and earth,
and of all that is, seen and unseen.

We believe this, and what follows, with a Faith that does not come from ourselves. It is Catholic Dogma that the eternal truths have been revealed to us by the Second Person of the Blessed Trinity, our Lord and Saviour Jesus Christ, the Word of God, while He was with us on earth, and that these truths can be believed only by a Faith that comes from God, and is infused into our soul by God in Baptism. It is for that reason that Catholics are requested to die for that Faith and for all the Dogmas it contains.

Here we express our supernatural Faith in the existence of God the Father, the first Person of the Blessed Trinity, the Creator of everything.

I believe in one Lord, Jesus Christ,
the only Son of God,
Eternally begotten of the Father.

God from God, Light from Light,
True God from true God.
Begotten, not made, of one being with the Father,
Through Him all things were made.
For us men and for our salvation
He came down from heaven.
By the power of the Holy Spirit
He became incarnate of the Virgin Mary and was made man.
For our sake He was crucified
under Pontius Pilate,
He suffered, died and was buried.
On the third day He rose again
in fulfillment of the Scriptures.
He ascended into heaven and is seated
at the right hand of the Father.
From there He shall come again in glory
to judge the living and the dead,
And His Kingdom will have no end.
I believe in the Holy Spirit,
the Lord and Giver of Life,
Who proceeds from the Father and the Son.
With the Father and the Son
He is worshipped and glorified,

He has spoken through the Prophets.
I believe in One Holy Catholic
and Apostolic Church.
I acknowledge one Baptism
for the forgiveness of sins.
I look for the resurrection of the dead,
And the Life of the world to come.
Amen.

Faith is intensely personal. For nearly two thousand years the Creed was said in the singular, "***I*** believe", since at death we will be judged on the strength of our personal belief in the Truths of the Catholic Church. It is very hard to know what other people believe and so it is very difficult to say "*we* believe", since the two faiths may not be the same. We do not know how prepared other Catholics are to die for the Faith of the Catholic Church. The way the Creed is said in ordinary Sunday Masses it sounds as a run-through like any other thoughtless routine.

After the public profession of Faith has been made, we come to the prayers of the faithful. In the great majority of cases they leave us comfortable in our selfish habits. For instance, when the reader invites us to pray for the Pope, it is invariable 'that he may lead and guide us on our journey', or words to that effect. It never occurs to them that that is precisely what the Holy Father does, so that, what we should be praying for is, that he may have a faithful flock which is prepared to listen to what he teaches and to implement it to the letter and in the Spirit.

And so it goes on. We pray 'that all may come to the Truth', and we forget to pray that they may come to the truth through the efforts, the constant prayers and the sacrifices offered up to God by the members of the Holy Catholic Church, the Mystical Body of Christ.

Yes, the Modernists, and all the priests who are so scared of them, have well padded us against any strenuous demands that ought to be made on us if we really believe what we professed in the Creed: ***"for us and for our salvation ... <u>He was crucified</u>...."*** Christ never instituted a Church that would leave Him alone in the way He showed us how the salvation of others is to be accomplished. He did institute a Church which says with St. Paul "***... and to do what I can in my own body to make up all***

that has still to be undergone by Christ for the sake of His Body the Church". (Col. 1:24).

Section Three (A)

The First of the Three Main Parts of the Mass

The Offertory

In order to fulfil the Sunday obligation, i.e. the obligation imposed on every Catholic to attend Mass devoutly on a Sunday, unless circumstances over which he has no control prevent this, a Catholic must be present in the church building *before* the start of the Offertory. Many Modernist priests who value the readings higher than the Consecration (although, like the Pharisees they are, they have no intention of living up to the readings) will of course dispute this. But Holy Church is a Mother and Her motherly rulings prevail.

The actions of the Offertory are simplicity itself. The Priest withdraws bread and wine from its profane use, i.e. from the normal function and use it has in the world to provide us with food and drink, and reserves them, "offers them", for God's exclusive use in providing us with 'food and drink' for the spiritual life of our soul on our journey on earth to our heavenly Fatherland. The act of withdrawing bread from its profane use of providing food in our daily lives to divine use for the spiritual Life of our souls is expressed by the following prayer:

Blessed are You, Lord, God of all creation.
Through Your goodness we have this bread to offer,
which earth has given and human hands have made.
It will become for us the Bread of Life.

By the *'Bread of Life'* here is meant the Body of Christ as It will become present to us at the highpoint of the Mass at the Consecration of the bread.

And the action by the Priest of withdrawing wine from its profane use in our daily lives to the exclusive use by God, is expressed by this prayer:

Blessed are You, Lord, God of all creation.
Through Your goodness we have this wine to offer,
Fruit of the vine and work of human hands,
It will become our Spiritual Drink.

By this 'Spiritual Drink' is meant of course the Blood of Christ, as it becomes present to us later on in the Mass at the Consecration of the wine.

The actions of the Offertory then may appear to us as being quite simple, but underneath them lie hidden for us some far-reaching, even awesome, realities.

For, in between these two prayers, the Priest does something else. At the side of the altar he lowers a few drops of water into the chalice containing the wine. These few drops completely disappear in the wine. In fact for all intents and purposes they become wine, and as such they too are offered up to God in the second of the above prayers.

Now herein lies that far-reaching, even awesome reality we spoke about above. For these few droplets of plain water in a strict sense represent the faithful present at this Mass, offering themselves. And in a wider sense these droplets represent the Church, the whole Body of Christ. These few droplets of water, indistinguishable from the wine once they have been lowered into the chalice, cease to be water at the moment of the Consecration of the wine and with the wine they too become the precious Blood of Our Lord and Saviour Jesus Christ.

What an honour! These few droplets of plain water make Christ's Sacrifice complete. For they allow Him to be the Head as they represent the faithful, His Body. And in the chalice, at the moment of the Consecration, the two combine together: the Head and the Body, to become once again "*The Perpetual Sacrifice*" of Calvary. In the Holy Mass prior to Vatican II we were free to kneel during the Offertory, and many did, for in a real sense the faithful present are watching the preparation <u>of their own execution</u>! What is being added to the chalice is they themselves, inexorably being turned into Victims at the moment of the Consecration. And no one watches his own execution sitting down as a non-participating spectator! The faithful, in union with the whole Church, find themselves present to each other and to Christ in the chalice for only one purpose: to offer themselves as true Victims as the Body of Our Lord to the Blessed Trinity as the one Perpetual Sacrifice of Calvary for the salvation of the world. They are in the most literal and unique sense 'Blood Brothers', for in the chalice the same

Blood is in them as is in Christ. There is no possible escape then: we are here at the heart and centre of the Universe. This must be the most momentous and precious Thing there is. Here the Church is most powerful and effective, for, after all, what can Christ refuse Her and us when we are together with Him in the Chalice? So it must be here that She is most under attack. The whole conspiracy of Modernism can only be geared to one thing: the abolition of the Perpetual Sacrifice, the Holy Catholic Mass!

No wonder, then, that in Sunday Masses the Holy Church wants Her children to be present at the Offertory.

All this explains the significance of the concluding prayer of the Offertory:

> May the Lord accept this Sacrifice at your hands,
> for the praise and glory of His Name,
> for our good, and the good of all His Church.

After the *Prayer over the Gifts* which is different for each Mass, and is to be found in every Sunday or weekday missal, we have arrived at the most important part of the Mass.

The Canon of the Mass

Most important, we said, because in the middle of the Canon of the Mass occurs the Consecration of the previously offered bread and wine. A more modern word in use for Canon is ***Eucharistic Prayer.***

There are four Eucharistic Prayers. The first of these is the translation from the Latin into the vernacular of the Canon which became universally used in Catholic Masses from the days of the Council of Trent, ca 1563, but had a much older beginning. The next two have been added to the Roman Liturgy by the Second Vatican Council (1962-1965) because of their venerable Tradition going back to the earliest times of Christianity. The fourth one is a Eucharistic Prayer cast in a modern form.

Whatever Eucharistic Prayer is used, they all start off with a *Preface*. Prefaces occur in important books to give some indication by the author of how the book is to be viewed. In the Preface to the Eucharistic Prayer the Church lays down how, what is to follow, must be understood in order that the faithful can be part of Her Mind. And the essential part of the Preface, and thus of the whole Eucharistic Prayer it introduces, is to give glory to God as expressed in these words:

The Lord be with you.
And also with you.
Lift up your hearts.
We have lifted them to the Lord.
Let us give thanks to the Lord our God.
It is right to give Him thanks and praise.
Father, all-powerful and ever-living God,
We do well *always* and *everywhere*
to give You thanks,
Through Jesus Christ Our Lord ...

If we truly understand the implications these words have on Catholic lives; if we truly mean what is being said here by us and in our name, we may begin to understand why Christ wants the members of the One Holy Church He founded to be present with Him in the chalice after the Consecration. For these words should lead those same members to the pinnacle of heroism....

Imagine a father and mother whose daughter has been abducted and murdered under the most gruesome circumstances. Not only are they required to fulfil Christ's demand of love, proclaimed by Him from Calvary in the new Covenant in His Blood, and sincerely forgive the perpetrators of such an evil act from their hearts. Here the way is opened for them to go much further. Here it is put to them to *always* and *everywhere* to give *thanks* to God, even in the terrible twist their life has taken. This demand can only be placed before people who have an unwavering Faith and Hope in God's absolute Holiness. Before people whom St. Peter refers to as *a chosen race, a holy priesthood, a consecrated nation, a people set apart to sing the praises of God* (1 Peter 2:9). This can only be addressed to people who believe that this absolute Holiness of God contains no flaw and can be trusted in the most trying circumstances of our lives.

Here the Preface of the Canon of the Mass sets the tone for us how to view the Consecration. For it is in the Consecration of the bread and wine that this absolute Holiness of God comes down on our altars in the Person of Jesus Christ, the Second Person of the Blessed Trinity, God from God, Holiness from Holiness.

Holy, holy, holy Lord,
God of power and might.
Heaven and earth are full of Your glory,
Hosanna in the highest.
Blessed is He who comes in the Name of the Lord,
Hosanna in the highest.

The Holiness of God.....

Most Christians would agree, at least in theory, that the Holiness of God must not be questioned. However that is still a far cry from the most necessary conviction that, on a Divine Command revealed to us, this Holiness should be unconditionally loved and trusted as something so perfect as to be totally flawless. The scramble for dollars and possessions in this life shows, that in practice even Catholics have their minds on other things, and that for them too the '*Beatitudes*' are worth at most an 'after hours number' so as not to interfere with the busy lines of 'business as usual' of the material life. It is for that reason that *greed* is called by St. Paul "*the same thing as worshipping a false god*" (Col. 3:5). Not so much because of Our Lord's realistic observation "*where your treasure is there your heart will be also*" (Luke 12:34). The much deeper reason for calling 'greed' "*the same thing as worshipping a false god*" is, because *greed* stands in direct relationship to the worst insult inherent in all Jewish idolatry: ***of safeguarding oneself against God.*** Of taking precautions against the Holiness of God Who hates any fortifications between Himself and His creatures, meant to give them a sense of security as if He cannot be trusted without them.

And now that the scramble for securities has reached fever-pitch and is now practised quite openly, even to the point of becoming murderous, then all those centuries of indifference to God, inherent in the West's idolatrous greed, thriving behind those futile barricades of money and possessions and weapons of mass destruction, have turned, according to the Book of Revelation of St. John, *into hatred of God.* Thus began the mass exodus from the Catholic Church, and with it the mass apostasy from the Catholic Faith. If the West could not be 'catholic' on its own idolatrous, greedy terms, then it had no intention of being Catholic on anyone else's terms, least of all on *His*....

The Holiness of God. Totally worthy of our trust without any fear of 'ulterior motives', secret designs or vindictiveness. To what degree of love could a human being be inspired by it if the human mind was free from suspicion or a defensive attitude.

The Holiness of God, capable of loving sinners; always to be trusted, never to be doubted, never to be queried, always worthy of our supernatural, infused, divine and Catholic *Hope*, the virtue that, <u>as is required here in the Preface of the Mass</u>, gives glory to God.

The mind simply boggles if it considered what our planet would look like, if people everywhere would let themselves be guided by a realistic acceptance of the *absolute Holiness of God.* And with this Preface, we must admit, the Holy Church has put us on the road to this perfection and has prepared us for the Consecration in a most suitable way.

Section Three (B)

The Second of the Three Main Parts of the Mass

The Consecration

A hush comes over the congregation. No matter how varied nowadays the beliefs are amongst Catholics of what is going to happen, everyone still agrees that it is a sacred moment.

We are told that the Priest is doing what Christ did at the Last Supper. "*While they were at Supper, Christ took some bread, said the blessing, broke the bread, and gave it to His disciples saying: 'Take this, all of you, and eat it. This is My Body which will be given up for you'.*" Immediately after having said these words and after having raised the sacred Host for the adoration of Christ by the faithful, the Priest himself genuflects as an act of adoration of Christ now present on the altar.

Now it is of the greatest importance that Catholics know and believe with all their heart, with all their mind and with all their Catholic Faith, that after the Priest has spoken these momentous words, <u>bread is no longer present on the altar</u>. At the Last Supper Christ could not have truthfully said *This is My Body* if what He was holding in His hands and gave to His Apostles was still bread. Christ's Body is ***not*** made of bread. So all that remains of bread is the appearance of it. The bread itself has gone and has been replaced by the Body of Christ. For Catholics this is such an Article of Faith that, if they do not believe this, they are no longer Catholic.

Since Christ's sacred Body in Heaven is alive, is united with His Blood, is united with His Soul and with His Divinity, all of this becomes present on the altar for our adoration after the words of the Consecration.

But Christ did much more than this at the Last Supper.

"*When supper was ended He took the cup. Again He gave you thanks and praise. He gave the cup to His disciples and said: 'Take this, all of you, and drink from it. This is the cup of My Blood, the Blood of the New and Everlasting Covenant. It will be shed for you and for all so that sins may be forgiven. Do this in memory of Me'.*"

What was said before applies here again. In order to remain faithful Catholics, all Catholics must believe with a firm Faith that after these words have been spoken over the wine, wine is no longer present in the chalice on the altar. It has been changed into the Blood of Christ. The appearance of wine is miraculously kept. The substance of wine has gone forever, just as the appearance of bread is miraculously kept with the host. The substance of bread too has gone forever.

But now there is a slight difference. Above it was said that after the Consecration of the bread, the *Body* of Christ is first and foremost present on the altar, and *with* it His sacred Blood, His Soul and His Divinity, since they are inseparable in Heaven. After the Consecration of the wine, what is first and foremost present in the chalice is the precious *Blood* of Christ, and *with* it His Body, His Soul and His Divinity. So the *whole* Christ is present under both appearances, but in a slightly different mode.

We have now arrived at the explanation of this great Mystery of our Catholic Faith: why, when instituting the Blessed Eucharist, did Christ insist on these different modes of presence in every Catholic Mass? His *Body* under the appearance of bread and concomitant with It His Blood, His Soul and His Divinity; and His precious *Blood* under the appearance of wine and concomitant with It His Body, His Soul and His Divinity.

Let us first meditate on Our Blessed Saviour's timing.

While they were at supper, Christ changed ordinary Jewish bread into His Body.

When supper was ended, Christ changed some of the table wine into His Blood.

There is here a distinct separation in time which is of the utmost significance. It creates the impression as if, through this separation in time, Christ wanted to impress on us the *separation* of His sacred Blood from His equally sacred Body.

When He spoke the words *This is My Body*, the substance of bread disappeared, and His sacred Body became present *as it was present sitting there at the table*, united with His Blood, His Soul and His Divinity. When, at the end of Supper, he said: *This is My Blood*, the substance of wine disappeared and in its place became present the Blood of Our Saviour *as it was present at that hour of the night*: united with His Body, His Soul and His Divinity. That night there was ***no*** separation between His Sacred Body and His Precious Blood.

What then is the reason for creating the impression of a separation, not only at that night but also in every Mass that would be said after this institution of the Blessed Eucharist *until the end of time*?

Christ knew what He was doing. At the Last Supper He could not give to His disciples and to His Church a mere mystical separation of His Body and Blood without an *actual* separation, not only in *time*, but also in *place*. And that actual separation of His Body and Blood took place the next day, when His bloodless Body was hanging on the Cross and His precious Blood was spilled all over Jerusalem for the forgiveness of the sins of all of mankind. And when He instituted the *mystical* separation of His Body and Blood at the Last Supper, He not only wrote out His own death warrant, He also signed it – as St. Paul says – "*with His Blood*". (Col. 2:15). He fully knew that by the Institution of the Blessed Eucharist He had made the *actual* separation of His

Body and Blood inevitable, and that from that moment on, it would merely be a matter of time, a matter of a few hours.

We may now start to understand why St. John wrote about the Last Supper "*in fine dilexit eos*": "*He loved them to the end*". He loved all His friends until there was nothing more to give. And this was given "*On the night He was betrayed...*"

"*A man can have no greater love than to lay down his life for his friends*".

At the Last Supper that was precisely what He did.

Every Christian knows that Christ's death on the Cross the next day was a real sacrifice. But how many know that already the Consecration at the Last Supper, separating His Body from His Blood, was just as much a real Sacrifice. For, in order that this mystical separation would be *real*, that Consecration made the shedding of His Blood inevitable. And it has linked every other Consecration to this atoning death on Calvary. For the very first Consecration consciously and inevitably made that link by making His death on the Cross inevitable. And by the words: "*Do this in memory of Me*", the link with

Calvary was extended for all times. At the Last Supper Christ was the real *Pascal Lamb* when He sacrificed Himself so that we may live. For it was at that precise moment that He made the actual separation of His Body and Blood mandatory. After that there was no escape.... There was nothing more to give....

It was for all the above mentioned reasons that the great Council of Trent (held from 1545 onwards) could define that the essence of the Catholic Mass is the re-enactment of the great Sacrifice of Calvary once again offered up to the Father but in an un-bloody manner. For that to be true, Our Lord's sacred Body and His precious Blood must be really and truly present on the altar in a kind of mystical separation, effected by the two Consecrations. And through the great Love of Christ shown at the Last Supper, that is exactly what is taking place. In this marvellous way Our Blessed Lord has made it possible that those who could not be present at His atoning death on Calvary can be present at the re-enactment of His death in the Mass, and to offer themselves up with their Head for the salvation of the whole world. And through this re-enactment of the great sacrifice on Calvary, every

Catholic Mass is a real sacrifice, because in this re-enactment the Mass truly renews what took place on Calvary.

Modernists hate this sacrificial aspect of the Catholic Mass. They want it to be a meal, a social event, where you can talk and laugh and sing and play music. But all faithful Catholics avoid such gatherings in the sure knowledge that the Catholic Mass once again offers up to the Father what was offered up to Him in the first Consecration at the Last Supper and on Calvary the next day.

Thus in the stillness that ought to be there, we can say the little prayer taken from the Divine Mercy Chaplet as taught by Our Lord to Blessed Sister Faustina Kowalska:

"Eternal Father, I offer You the Body and Blood, Soul and Divinity of Your dearly beloved Son, Our Lord Jesus Christ, for the atonement of our own sins, and of those of the whole world".

After the Consecration, in the second half of the Eucharistic Prayer, the Catholic faithful present at this Mass join in with the Universal Church in giving glory and thanks to God and in praying for the needs of all Christians. All four Eucharistic Prayers address God the Father immediately after the Consecration. The tone is one of joy and gratitude for the universal Redemption won by Christ in His Sacred Passion and Death as well as through the offering of this Mass. This joy persists even if we too have to suffer in some way in order to be part of this great Sacrifice, and even when we may be asked to lay down our lives in times of persecution. For it is here that all Christian men, women and children ask for, and obtain, the necessary love and strength.

That this is a serious matter we know from what St. John wrote for the whole Church in the 13th chapter of his *Book of Revelation* or the *Apocalypse.* How, during the reign of the beast, Antichrist will be allowed to make war on the Saints *and conquer them* for 42 months. For St. John here, the Saints are all those who are in State of Grace through their unwavering Faith in God and their firm resolve ***not*** to do evil. Three-and-a-half years is a long time....

No wonder, then, that Our Holy Mother the Catholic Church wants all Her children to be present at the Sunday Mass. There, in union with Christ, they are offered up to the Father for the whole of the coming week, *so that sins may be for-*

given, and Good may be allowed to flourish and gain its rightful place in all humanity.

Every Eucharistic Prayer ends with the great Doxology or formula for liturgical praise to the Blessed Trinity:

"Through Him, with Him, in Him, in the unity of the Holy Spirit, all glory and honour is Yours, Almighty Father, for ever and ever."

To which the whole congregation gives its assent with a resounding Amen.

Section Three (C)

The Third of the Three Main Parts of the Mass

Holy Communion

This part is enormously rich in ritual and Tradition both in the Old and in the New Testament.

In the *Old Testament* we read what God had ordained the Jews to do prior to their Exodus from Egypt.

> The Lord said to Moses and Aaron in the land of Egypt,
>
> "This month shall be for you the beginning of months; it shall be the first month of the year for you. Tell all the congregation of Israel that on the tenth day of this month they shall take every man a lamb one for each family, a lamb for each household. If the household is too small for a lamb, then a man must join with his neighbour next to his house as the number of

persons requires. You must take into account what each person can eat in deciding the number for the animal.

Your lamb shall be without blemish, a male a year old; you shall take it from the sheep or from the goats; and you shall keep it until the fourteenth day of this month, when the whole assembly of the congregation of Israel shall kill their lambs in the evening. Then they shall take some of the blood, and put it on the two doorposts and the lintel of the houses in which they eat them. They shall eat the flesh that night, roasted; with unleavened bread and bitter herbs they shall eat it. Do not eat any of it raw or boiled with water, but roasted, its head with its legs and its inner parts. And you shall let none of it remain until the morning, anything that remains until the morning you shall burn.

In this manner you shall eat it: your loins girded, your sandals on your feet, and your staff in your hand; and you shall eat it in haste. It is the Lord's Passover. For I will pass through the land of Egypt that night, and I will strike down all the first-born in the land of Egypt, both man

> and beast; and on all the gods of Egypt I will execute judgments: I am the Lord. The blood shall serve to mark the houses where you are; and when I see the blood, I will pass over you, and no plague shall fall upon you to destroy you, when I strike the land of Egypt". (Book of Exodus, 12:1-13).

It is not hard to see what God had in Mind when He ordered the sons of Israel to slaughter and *eat* the first pascal lambs. And the lamb's blood on the doorpost and the lintel above the door is a sign of salvation. "*When I see the blood I shall pass over you, and you shall escape the destroying plague....*"

All this was in preparation of the atoning Death of the true *Lamb of God*, Our Lord and Saviour Jesus Christ. At the Last Supper, *and* as a consequence of what Our Lord did there, the next day on Calvary, Christ became the True Pascal Lamb that must now be eaten. This we not only have on the authority of the Old Testament as explained in the above-quoted passage from the Book of Exodus, but on the even stronger authority of Our Lord Himself in the

New Testament as quoted in the Gospel of St. John in the 6th chapter.

The day after Our Blessed Lord had fed a crowd of five thousand from a mere five loaves and two fishes on the far side of the Sea of Tiberias, the Jews went looking for Him. When they found Him on their side of the lake they said:

"Rabbi, when did you come here?" Jesus answered them,

> "*I tell you most solemnly, you are not looking for Me because you have seen the signs, but because you ate your fill of the loaves.*
> *Do not work for the food that cannot last,*
> *but work for the food that endures to eternal life,*
> *the kind of food the Son of Man is offering you;*
> *for on Him the Father, God Himself, has set his seal.*"
>
> Then they said to him, "What must we do, if we are to do the works that God wants?" To this Jesus replied,
>
> "*This is working for God, that you believe in the One He has sent.*"

So they said to him, "Then what sign will you give to show us that we should believe in You? What work will You do? Our fathers ate the manna in the wilderness; as it is written, 'He gave them bread from heaven to eat'."

Jesus then said to them,

"I tell you most solemnly it was not Moses who gave you the bread from heaven;

it is My Father who gives you the true Bread from heaven. For the Bread of God is that

which comes down from heaven,

and gives life to the world."

They said to him, "Lord, give us this Bread always." Jesus said to them,

"I am the Bread of Life.

He who comes to Me will never go hungry,

and he who believes in Me will never thirst.

But, as I told you,

you can see Me and still do not believe.

All that the Father gives Me will come to Me;

and whoever comes to Me

I shall not turn him away;

for I have come down from heaven,

not to do My own will,

but to do the will of the One who sent Me.
And this is the will of the One who sent Me,
that I should lose nothing
of all that He has given to Me,
but that I raise it up on the last day.
Yes, this is the will of My Father,
that every one who sees the Son and believes in Him
shall have eternal life;
and that I shall raise him up on the last day."

The Jews then commenced complaining to each other about Him because he had said, "I am the bread that came down from heaven." They said, "Surely this is Jesus, the son of Joseph. We know His father and mother. How can He now say, 'I have come down from heaven'?" Jesus answered them,

"*Stop complaining amongst yourselves.*
No one can come to Me
unless he is drawn by the Father who sent Me.
and I will raise him up on the last day.
It is written in the prophets,
'*And they will all be taught by God*.'
To hear the teaching of the Father

and learn from it,
is to come to Me.
Not that any one has seen the Father
except the One who comes from God;
He has seen the Father.
I tell you most solemnly
whoever believes has eternal life.
I am the Bread of Life.
Your fathers ate the manna in the desert,
and they are dead.
This is the Bread that comes down from heaven,
so that a man may eat it and not die.
I am the living Bread which has come down from heaven.
Anyone who eats this Bread will live forever;
and the Bread that I shall give
is My flesh for the life of the world."
Then the Jews started arguing among themselves,
"How can this man give us his flesh to eat?" they said.
Jesus replied,
"*I tell you most solemnly,*
unless you eat the Flesh of the Son of Man

and drink His Blood,
you will not have Life in you.
Anyone who eats My flesh and drinks My blood
has eternal life,
and I shall raise him up on the last day.
For My Flesh is real food
and My Blood is real drink.
He who eats My Flesh and drinks My Blood
lives in Me, and I live in him.
As the living Father sent Me,
and I draw Life from the Father,
so he who eats Me will draw Life from Me.
This is the Bread which came down from heaven,
not like the bread our ancestors ate,
they are dead.
But anyone who eats this Bread will live forever."

He taught this doctrine at Capernaum, in the synagogue.

Many of his disciples, when they heard it, said, "This is intolerable language. How can anyone accept it?" Jesus was aware that his followers were complaining about it and said,

"*Does this upset you?*

What if you see the Son of Man ascend to where He was before?
It is the spirit that gives life,
the flesh has nothing to offer.
The words I have spoken to you are Spirit and Life" …
"*This is why I told you that no one can come to Me*
unless it is granted him by the Father."
After this many of his disciples left Him and stopped going with Him. Then Jesus said to the Twelve,
"*What about you? Do you want to go away too?*"
Simon Peter answered, "Lord, <u>who shall we go to</u>? You have the words of eternal Life, and we believe; we know that You are the Holy One of God". (John 6:26-69).

And that is the same answer we can give Our Lord in Holy Communion.

The text quoted from St. John's Gospel is a long one. But it really says everything that there is to say. The Promise of the Blessed Eucharist made by Our Lord in the synagogue at Capernaum was in a most literal sense fulfilled at the Last Supper, when He gave those who had followed Simon Peter's profession of Faith and had stayed with Him, His own Body to eat and His own Blood to drink in their first Holy Communion. If only the Jews in the synagogue of Capernaum had shared the Faith of St. Peter, they too would have come to see how easy it was for the Son of God to fulfil His Promise and to give His Body as food and His Blood to drink in Holy Communion.

Now that the time for this has arrived, the usual prayer said by Christians before a meal, is now said:

Our Father who art in Heaven
Hallowed be Thy Name;
Thy Kingdom come;
Thy Will be done on earth as it is in Heaven.
Give us this day our daily bread;
And forgive us our trespasses
As we forgive those who trespass against us.
And lead us not into temptation,
But deliver us from evil.

Since Holy Communion in a Catholic Mass is a Sacrament of the Living, that is, a Sacrament exclusively for those in state of Grace, those conscious of a mortal sin which has not been forgiven in private, oral Confession to a Priest of the Catholic Church, would commit a grave sin of sacrilege if they went to Communion in state of mortal sin. Saying a hurried 'Act of Contrition' at this moment is ***not*** sufficient. The terrible habit of the Modernists in introducing the widespread use of general absolution has wreaked havoc in countless souls and consciences. The Penitential Rite at the start of the Mass does ***not*** forgive unconfessed mortal sins. The greatest erosion of the spiritual life in Catholics has been brought about by the thoughtless practice of receiving Holy Communion in state of mortal sin. It is especially here, in this whole area of *self-absolution,* that Catholics who indulge in this practice have raised their 'consciences' to an absolute above the absolute moral order instituted by God. This intolerable situation has been pointed out as an abuse by the Holy Father, Pope John Paul II, to the bishops of Australia in their '*ad limina*' visit in December 1998.

The above reminder is necessary in order to understand what follows next.

We have arrived at the moment in the Mass where the Peace that only Christ can give is extended to us from the living Christ, the "*Prince of Peace*", present on the altar. Catholics who out of human respect are prepared to commit a further mortal sin by receiving Holy Communion in state of mortal sin cannot possibly receive this Peace that only Christ can give. No 'handshake', 'kiss of peace' or wafting 'peace' around can make up for that. Only Christ can give that peace. But it is most certainly extended to those who, like the repentant tax collector in the Gospel, humble themselves before God, admit their unworthiness to receive Holy Communion, and ask for forgiveness and for the grace of a good confession in the near future. Their non-participation in receiving Holy Communion is the very means by which such forgiveness is extended to them with the Peace of Christ.

St. Paul reminds us in one of his letters of the seriousness of eating the Lord's Body when not distinguishing it from profane bread.

> Anyone who eats this Bread or drinks the Cup of the Lord unworthily, shall be guilty of the Body and of the Blood of the Lord.
> Everyone is to examine himself before eating this Bread and drinking this Cup, because anyone who eats and drinks without recognising the Body, is eating and drinking his own condemnation. That is why many of you are weak and ill, and why some of you have died. If only we examined ourselves, we should not be punished like that. But when the Lord does punish us like that, it is to correct us in order to prevent us from being condemned with the world.
> (1 Cor. 11: 27-32).

"*....without recognising the Body....*" Here St. Paul touches on the essence of the Blessed Eucharist. If Catholics go up thinking they can go in any state they like in the understanding that all they are receiving is a mere piece of bread, but ***not*** the Body of Our Lord Jesus Christ, "*....they are eating and drinking their own condemnation,* if they receive the Body of Our Lord in state of mortal sin. And how many Catholic children when leaving their Catholic schools *do recognise the Body*?

The Priest too who says the Mass recognises the gravity of the moment when he prays:

> Lord Jesus Christ,
> With Faith in Your Love and Mercy,
> I eat Your Body and drink Your Blood.
> Let it not bring me condemnation,
> But health in mind and body.

The words "*condemnation*", "*health*", refer directly to what St. Paul wrote to the Corinthians in the above-quoted passage: "*That is why many of you are weak and ill*", which means 'unhealthy', because "*without recognising the Body....*" "*they are eating and drinking their own condemnation*".

From the seriousness of, and the divine punishments attached to, the malpractices in receiving Holy Communion, Catholics are able to measure the enormous graces the Lord has in store for those who receive His Body and Blood worthily. They are so numerous that there will never come an end to enumerating them.

Graces of Faith, Hope and Love. Graces of fortitude and strength. Graces in the reception of the Seven Gifts of the Holy Spirit. Graces of Holy Purity by which we "*see God*". Graces by which are removed from us all that we cannot take with us to Heaven. Graces of conversion of all those we stand in for. The list is endless.

Why? Because within us is one of the greatest gifts of them all: *the Sacred Heart of Jesus*. And within that storehouse are contained all the treasures of heaven and earth: the treasures of His Humanity and His Divinity. The rubies of His Blood, the diamonds of His tears, the pearls of His sweat, the gold of His infinite Love, lavished on those who love Him. And these treasures we can offer up to Our Lady for safekeeping out of gratitude for all She has done for us in bringing Him down from Heaven. For it is through Her that Marian Catholics become Eucharistic Catholics.....

One day we can receive Him as our Father. On other days we can welcome Him as our Friend, our Brother, our Redeemer, our Lawyer, our Teacher, our Doctor, our Priest and our Sacrifice. The list is as long as are our imagination and love.

This is the Lamb of God
Who takes away the sins of the world.
Blessed are those who are called to His supper.
Lord, I am not worthy to receive You,
But only say the word and I shall be healed.

Truly, what can He refuse us now? And what can we refuse Him?

And with this we leave the Catholic soul in profound contemplation with its God and in enduring thanksgiving.

Epilogue

That which should be read last

And so, at the end of this little book, we once again have made our way into the presence of Her, whom sinner and Saint, in agony and ecstasy, has graced with the ever-lasting name: *Our Holy Mother the Catholic Church.* For it was exclusively to Her, that Her Groom and Her Head, Our Lord and Saviour Jesus Christ, had entrusted the continuation of His Perpetual Sacrifice, the Holy Catholic Mass.

Like Our Lady, the Church grew in years, but never wrinkled. She is still the youthful, spotless Bride of the Lamb of God, the Holy One, the Faithful One. Over the centuries She has done what Her Divine Founder and Groom wanted Her to do: to bear Him children, many children, to fill His Father's House from the ends of the earth. She instructed them in purity of doctrine, in poverty of spirit, in obedience to God's Word. And the Son of God loved Her. He adorned Her with His most precious jewels; He entrusted to Her care His priceless possessions: His Body, His Blood, His Grace, His

Heart, His Truth, His Infinite Mercy, the Mysteries of His Divine Knowledge, the Honour of His Holy Mother. He cared for Her as never a groom cared for his bride. And in return the Church loved the Lamb of God with an eternity of Love. For Him She loved the sinner as much as the Saint. She taught the ignorant as well as the learned. She strengthened the Martyr to stand firm till the end; She consoled the bereaved, prepared the dying and cared for the poor and the sick, the orphan and the widow, the heathen and the lost. She was all to all.

The Church will never be under the control of iniquity nor under the command of men. She can live under any system, outlast any enemy, survive any evil. For the Church does not rest on human counsels, nor on the councils of this world. Her Head is Divine, so is Her Life. She has no need to speak with the voice of this world to be heard.

For within Her is the pearl of great beauty for which the merchant-in-the-know sacrificed everything in order to possess it: *Catholic Faith*, the most priceless gift of Almighty God to finite little man. For it is through that Faith, and that Faith alone, that we know Him, the Father Almighty, and His

Son, and His Holy Spirit, His Mother, His Church, and the bodily presence of His Son in the Blessed Eucharist; His Face in the poor, and His Truth in "*Humanae Vitae*"....

That Catholic Faith will never die on this earth. It will never disappear from this earth. It will never cease to have consequences on this earth. Fruits of redemption and eternal salvation. Fruits of prayer and penance, of great Hope and great Love. Fruits of conversion to Her through Whom we received it in the first place: our *Holy Mother, the Catholic Church!*

But in the caring for the children of the Lamb of God, there grew in Her own heart but one desire, a desire so secret that it never left the place where it was born for fear that it would be revealed. But against Her will the desire grew, and finally the Bridegroom read it in Her eyes, the unspoken secret between them in the intimate union of their Mystical Life. She loved the Lamb of God; She had studied Him in His Life on earth; She understood His every mood. She had seen His Birth, and imitated His poverty. She had seen His Hidden Life, and imitated His Obedience and Love for His Parents. She had followed Him in His travels whilst preaching the Kingdom of God, and Her own missionaries had gone out to the four corners of the earth. The union of love between the Bridegroom and His Bride had grown strong and in the chaste intimacy between the Son of God and His Catholic Church, the secret could no longer be kept. Had not St. Paul compared the union of the Christian marriage to the union between Christ and His Church? And the Creator of Christian Marriage understood....

Faithfully, His Bride had taught every young bride that came before Her altar to be joined in holy wedlock 'to have her man and to hold': to hold on to him for better or worse, to follow him wherever he may go. To suffer with him whatever would be his fate. And the Church watched them go.... And the desire in Her own heart grew stronger. Would She alone, in all Eternity, be a Bride, espoused to a Man who for love of Her let Himself be crucified, without having shared the experience with Him? Would She alone not be allowed to show Her love '*in fine*': till the very end? Would she alone be the only Bride not knowing what it is: '*exinanivit Semetipsum*', 'He emptied Himself'? She had seen Him in His agony,

She had watched Him being scourged, crowned with thorns, mocked, spat upon, rejected. She had meditated on His last journey on earth, carrying His Cross all the way to Calvary out of Love for Her; seen His final, all-embracing Sacrifice, laying down His life for His sheep, and how His holy Mother shared every suffering with Him. And the Love in Her own heart became infinite....If only somehow, somehow, She could do the same, share with Him, show Her love for Him and for Her children, *their* children, to the same extent: 'in fine'. For every Martyr She had sustained, his hour had finally arrived. Would *Her Hour* ever come? To suffer the indignity of seeing Barabbas preferred to Her? To hear Herself being condemned to death, and then at last be permitted to follow in the bleeding footsteps of the Man She had adored in so much love? All the way to Her own execution, Her own annihilation? To give Her life for Him. She had faithfully imitated His every example. Would oh would there be given Her, before the End, ONE chance, Her chance, to pay Him back; to imitate Him 'in fine', till the end....

And the Father of all understood. And in His infinite Wisdom and Love, He found a way...

The Jewish leaders once said amongst themselves: "We don't like this Christ and His message. We want one in our own image, a message to our own liking". They did not like the Messiah as sent by God and promised by the Prophets. He had to be 'improved'. He had to be 'renewed'. As He was, He had to be done away with. And when they had finished remodelling Him 'after their own image and liking', *He had to be buried....* On the Cross He had become their image. He finally looked like them, as they were known to the Father: disfigured and killed by Sin. But only then was the great miracle being wrought: through His frightful Passion and Death, sustained by an Infinite Love, *they themselves, not Him, had been renewed, redeemed!* In the Heavenly Beauty of the Supernatural Life, they could look again as the adopted children of God, in true likeness of His Son Jesus Christ. And out of His pierced Heart, washed in His water and Blood, the new creation was born: His Church, His very own Bride.

As the latest in a long line of break-aways down history, 'Modern Man' too has raised his voice to God, and said:

> *"We don't like this Catholic Church as handed down to us through the ages. We want Her changed. We want Her renewed after our own image. Her message, we want it changed after our own liking, along the beautiful lines of a Teilhard de Chardin, who allows us to embrace the world."*

And God saw the pitiful state to which 'evolution' has reduced 'modern man': '*an irrational animal, let loose in nature, groping his way through endless trial and error, because he doesn't know enough history, enough religion, enough prayer*' (Lammerts). And remembering the dearest wish of His Son's Bride on earth and remembering the true renewal: Redemption, that had been brought about by the Death of His Son on the Cross, He relented.

"And their cries gained the upper hand ..." (Lk. 23:23)

The hour of the Church had finally come.

Which then reveals the most obvious purpose of the One-World 'Church', the teilhardian 'church of darkness': to be the harlot church, the 'Barabbas', preferred by 'modern man' in preference to the spotless Bride of the Lamb of God, our Holy Mother the Catholic Church. And the fury of hell unleashed against the Catholic Church will then be such, that St. John could write in his Apocalypse with reference to 'the Beast',

"And it was given to it to make war with the Saints *and to conquer them...*"

But the Catholic Church will not die out altogether. Not all the Catholics will be annihilated. But their hidden existence will eclipse the Church for a while, like the stone before the Holy Sepulchre hid for a while that other Sacred Body of Our Lord. They will be hidden in the New Ark, the Marian Dimension, carrying them safely over the Deluge of Terror unleashed on earth during the reign of the Beast. The Good Friday of the Church will be terrible, but the One Who sustained Her Son on the day of His Crucifixion, has now been officially appointed by the Second Vatican Council to sustain the Church on Hers.

For the Bride of the Lamb of God, and out of love for that same sinful humanity that crucified Her Groom, the same hour has at last arrived. Now His Bride wishes to go through the same experience, through the same Good Friday, for the sake of 'modern man': that pathetic end-product of a faked evolution.

Is that a crime? Is that so confusing? Does that make Her weak? So that we should be ashamed of Her, go our own way, calling ourselves 'Christians' and no longer Catholic? Does that give us the right to push Her aside, follow our own 'beliefs' and passions, because the Church no longer seems to know what She is doing?

The time and the hour has come, that the world will select the 'harlot': the teilhardian 'church of darkness' in preference to Her. So that the Church can suffer what Christ went through when that same humanity cast Him aside in preference for a robber and murderer. And then at last will the Catholic Church be able to show Her love for God and men 'in fine', till the end. And go the same painful way to Her own Calvary. But just like Her Groom, the Church is still beautiful and infinitely powerful. She will rise again and conquer the earth, because a Church in such Love is the most powerful thing on earth: irresistible.

There are many silent, timid, confused bishops. They are wounding the Church, oh yes. The Church feels it, like Christ did. Christ suffered. So does His Church. For the vast teilhardian 'church of darkness', in its thirst for power over the Catholic Church, is, as the Second Beast of the Apocalypse, actively engaged in hastening the global enslavement under Antichrist. But when this harlot-church will be handed over to 'the Beast' to make it appear as if finally Antichrist and Satan are ruling over the Catholic Church, when they dominate this vast, one-world anti-church with its anti-pope, then the *machinery* of the Catholic Church may appear to be there under their control. But the Bride of the Lamb of God will be safely under the protection of Her, appointed by God at this Her hour, to be the Mother of the Church.

And when the Church knows what it is 'to be the Bride of the Lamb of God', then the same conquering Powers will make Her irresistible to the powers and forces of Darkness. At the moment of Her greatest desertion and seeming annihilation, She will prove to be the true Daughter of God the Father: indestructible. And if we will be proud of Her then, we must be proud of Her now. If we will be proud to be called Her Catholic children then, and flock to Her in love, we should stay with Her now, in Her moment of greatest desertion, when She needs all of us most.

> "For She is a breath of the Majesty of God,
> Pure emanation of the Glory of the Almighty,
> Hence nothing impure can touch Her.
> She is the reflection of the Eternal Light,
> Untarnished mirror of God's active Power,
> The image of His Perfection.
> Although alone, She can do all,
> Herself unchanging, She makes all things new.
> In each generation She enters into holy souls,
> Forming them into friends of God and prophets.
> For God loves only those who live with Wisdom.
> She is indeed more splendid than the sun,
> She outshines all the constellations.
> Compared with light, She takes precedence.
> For light must yield to night,
> But over Wisdom evil will never triumph!
> She deploys Her strength from one end of the earth to the other:
> It is She who orders all things for good"
>
> (Wisdom 7:25 – 8:1)

So there She is Our Holy Mother the Catholic Church created by God in the image and likeness of His Holy Mother, the Blessed Virgin Mary. It is this Faith, this sure knowledge, *which is the foundation of the Hope* with which the Catholic Church enters the most crucial times of Her existence. And as this little booklet has been at pains to explain, this Faith, this Hope and this Love are fed and greatly strengthened in all Her children in where She is most Our Mother, in the Catholic Mass.

Part II

The Fruits of the Catholic Mass

The Descent of the Holy Spirit and the Power of the Blessed Virgin Mary

The Fruits of the Catholic Mass are inexhaustible. Because they lead to eternal life, and eternal life has no end, the graces of the Mass are infinite. They truly are "*the fountain of water inside him, welling up to eternal life*" (John 4:14).

The graces of even one Catholic Mass exceed the heights which the greatest Saints have scaled and extend further into the past and into the future than even the most daring thoughts can comprehend. The reasons for this I have set out in Part I above to which the reader is referred to avoid unnecessary repetitions.

However, for a good understanding of what is to follow, mention must be made here of one person who was not present in the Cenacle when, during the Last Supper, Our Lord and Saviour Jesus Christ changed bread and wine into His own Body and Blood, and when He commanded his first Priests and Bishops "*to do this as a memorial of Me*". Here we refer of course to the Mother of the Lamb of God at the very moment that Her Son "*laid down His life for His sheep*" when He signed His own death warrant. For, with the institution of the Blessed Eucharist, that is, with the mystical separation of His Body and Blood, Our Saviour had made the *real* separation inevitable. So great had been His Love for us that He made the avoidance of the Cross the next day impossible.

And now the Lord had gone, ascended to His Father after His mission had been accomplished. And the disciples returned to the Upper Room, but this time Mary, the Mother of Jesus was with them:

> "So from the Mount of Olives as it is called, they went back to Jerusalem, a short distance away, no more than a sabbath walk; and when they reached the city they went to the upper room where they were staying ... All these joined in continuous prayer, together with several women, including Mary, the Mother of Jesus, and with His brothers." (Acts, 1:12-14).

On the encouragement which St. Ignatius has built into his world famous Thirty Day retreat, we may devotedly meditate on the thoughts that at this moment must have passed through the mind of the Immaculate Conception. Her mission had not yet come to an end. She still had a role to play in the formation of the early Church, guiding the steps of those who had been appointed by Her Son to guide the steps of others.

They were all Her children, born into the Mystical Body of Christ, of which Her Son was the head and She Herself had been the beginning, when, as the sole member at the time, She gave Her consent at the Incarnation. According to St. Paul, it had been ordained from all eternity that the Son of God would redeem the world *as the Head of a Body*. So, in order that He could be a Head at His coming, the Holy Virgin Mary was asked to supply Him not only with a physical body that made Him human, but also with His Mystical Body that made Him Head. And since at the Incarnation of the Son of God, there were no St. Peter, St. John or a St. Paul, She was the only one to give Her consent, and thus, as the Holy Church teaches, She was, as the sole member of the Mystical Body of Christ, the beginning of the Church, the *Mediatrix of all Graces*, and the only

Mother of all the children who would eventually be born into supernatural Life from that union between Her and Her Head. Just as all the members of the human race are children of Eve, born from the union between herself and her head, Adam.

Now it is inconceivable that St. Paul would know more about these deep and consoling truths then the one who had been asked to make the decision that this Church would ever come into existence. And once Her consent had been given, then the *fullness of grace* conceived within Her and born from Her made Her the *Mediatrix of all Graces* that would eventually be poured out over all mankind (Popes *Leo XIII* and *St. Pius X*).

Our Lady had not been ordained a Priest, and She was fully aware of the deep significance of this. No woman, in the full knowledge that she has a female body, can stand at the moment of the Consecration *in persona Christi* and say "*This is my (male) body*". It would be a lie at the most holy moment in the universe and would make the whole act totally ineffectual. Thus She depended on the Apostles to receive the Body of Her Lord and Son in Holy Communion. Only to Her, the Mediatrix of all

Graces, had it been given to see the full extent to which the Graces from the Cross would flow from the pierced Heart of Her Son in every Mass. No one can *mediate* what he has no knowledge of. Which means that a mediator must be in the possession of <u>all</u> the facts, and that the Mediatrix of <u>all</u> the graces must be in the possession of every purpose for which the mediated graces are given. And we stress once again that all these graces mediated by the Blessed Virgin Mary flow from the Cross and from the re-enactment of that great Sacrifice, the Catholic Mass.

Thus it was imperative that the descent of the promised Holy Spirit on the assembled Church in the Upper Room would be implored from the Blessed Trinity by the offering up of the daily Mass and daily Holy Communion. We can therefore imagine that Our Lady observed proceedings with a watchful eye and if there was any neglect in understanding on the part of the Apostles, that She would fulfill Her role as Mediatrix, and see to it that Peter and John understood. She was not in the position to direct the Church, only to mediate the graces from Her Head to obtain the desired effect. And if there was anything lacking in the leaders of that Church, She would supply the so necessary understanding and follow-up. She may have used words such as these:

> *"Our Lord and Saviour has gone to His Father in Heaven and so you can no longer depend on Him to do what He commissioned you to do in memory of Him in this very Upper Room: <u>the breaking of the Bread</u>. There are many assembled here with us who depend on you to do what He told you to do in His Name: <u>to change bread and wine into His own Body and Blood</u> and to give them Holy Communion.*
>
> *As you are aware, before He ascended to His place at the right Hand of God the Father, He promised that "<u>you, not many days from now, will be baptised by the Holy Spirit</u>" (Acts, 1:5).*
>
> *What better preparation for this coming could we find than the daily breaking of Bread in the Holy Eucharist and to let the Lord implore the Father*

> *for this coming from our altar and from our hearts?"*

If these noble thoughts had occurred to the Apostles without the prompting of the Blessed Virgin Mary, they would still, as real Graces, have been mediated for them by Her as the Mediatrix of all Graces. As we know now, this preparation for the coming of the Holy Spirit took nine days and thus could conceivably have been a coming prompted, or even hastened, by a Novena of Nine Masses.

That Our Lady has the power *to hasten God's Hour* is a truth solidly based on scriptural evidence. We can see this power at work during the wedding feast at Cana and in the acceptance in the state of Sanctifying Grace of John the Baptist by the Incarnate Son of God some three months before his circumcision while he was still in his mother's womb.

> "His birth brought great rejoicing. Even in the womb he leapt for joy, so near was man's salvation." (Preface of St. John the Baptist)

Mary's eagerly looking forward to the daily reception of Her divine Son in Holy Communion taught St. John the Evangelist and indeed all of us a valuable lesson. By Her example, her prayers and Her power of intercession it has become quite clear to the Holy Catholic Church that those of Her children who have found the treasure of a great devotion to the Mother of God become Her Eucharistic children. And the first of these was St. John. Love of the Blessed Virgin Mary, far from eclipsing (as the Modernists so avidly hold up) devotion due to God, leads to frequent Mass attendance and to the reception of Holy Communion. And the ever-increasing descent of the Holy Spirit on these true children of Mary has its origin in the Cenacle where the coming of the Holy Spirit was hastened by the foresight of His power employed by Her who had become His Bride at the Incarnation.

Thus a great love for Our Lady, a great love for the Holy Catholic Faith and for Our Lord in the Blessed Eucharist, the outpouring of the Gifts of the Holy Spirit, of which Wisdom is the first and the most important, and lives free from sin and delusion, are among the greatest Fruits of the Holy Sacrifice of the Mass.

> "May you walk in His Ways, always knowing what is right and good, until you enter your heavenly inheritance."
>
> (Third solemn blessing on the feast day of the Triumph of the Cross, September 14).

But, as if the foregoing was not enough, there are innumerable other graces to be obtained from what was instituted by Christ at the Last Supper and completed the next day on Calvary, the Fruits of which are impossible to count, for they are truly infinite.

"... and keep them alive in famine"

One of these Fruits we come across in the Liturgy of the Sacred Heart. There, in the Entrance Antiphon we are told:

"The thoughts of His Heart last through every generation, that He will rescue them from death and keep them alive in time of famine."

To keep them supernaturally alive in the time of a great drought of the Word of God as we experience today in every corner of the globe; and to keep them naturally alive when we experience a great famine of food, as is being prepared by Monsanto and its facilitators in Governments also for every corner of the globe.

"Behold, the days are coming", says the Lord God, "when I will send a famine on the land; not a famine of bread, nor a thirst for water, but of hearing the words of the Lord. They shall wander from sea to sea, and from north to east; they shall run to and fro, to seek the word of the Lord, but they shall not find it." (Amos 8:11-12).

The first victims of this terrible drought are those who created it, the Modernists, that is those who succeeded in their untiring efforts to make many Catholics accept *as Catholic* all the *modern* heresies away from Catholic teaching.

"Alas for you, scribes and Pharisees, you hypocrites! For you travel over sea and land to make a single proselyte, and when you have him you make him twice as fit for hell as you are yourselves." (Mt. 23:15).

And who are the ones who are destined to survive this severe drought and its terrible consequences?

> "Blessed is the man who trusts in the Lord, whose trust is the Lord. He is like a tree planted by water, that sends out its roots by the stream, and does not fear when heat comes, for its leaves remain green, and is not anxious in the year of drought, for it does not cease to bear fruit." (Jer. 17:8)

There are two ways open to Satan to make Catholics 'adore' his seed, Antichrist.

One way is to make those 'of little Faith and trust in God' so anxious that they capitulate to him by accepting "*the mark of the beast*" for fear of not being able "*to buy and sell*" food, and so face the prospect of dying of starvation.

The other way is to starve them spiritually by making them follow the tortuous roads by which the Modernists enter the One-World 'Church of Darkness' through their acceptance of "*the mark of the beast*".

The prospect of spiritual 'death by starvation' of Catholics is all too real going by the vast numbers that have left the Catholic Church in order to enter the easy church, held up everywhere by Modernism and immorality. The answer to this is the acquisition of much Light and an over-abundance of spiritual life through the possession of that *fountain of Grace welling up to eternal Life.* We know where that fountain is to be found: in the thoughts of His Heart, lasting through every generation, that He will "rescue them from death".

We also know where that Heart is present on this earth and where we receive It.

This takes care of the first part of the Entrance Antiphon on the Feast day of the Sacred Heart: that, from generation to generation, He will rescue His elect from spiritual death, a death in time of starvation caused by a drought of the Word of God. This rescue must imply that this terrible drought will ***not*** extend to His elect. The Word of God as spoken through His Church will never be lacking to those who combine the supernatural insights of their strong Catholic Faith with the natural understanding of what is going on on this earth. To this golden combination Pope St. Pius X referred when he gave it the name of *discipline of the mind*. Natural understanding enlightened by the supernatural insights of a strong and a cherished Catholic Faith, and supernatural insights enriched by a good understanding of how this Faith is to be lived while here on earth.

> "May you walk in His Ways, always knowing what is right and good, until you enter your heavenly inheritance."

There is no doubt about it: Satan will succeed in frightening many lukewarm Catholics into submission with the fear that they may not be able "*to buy and sell*" (Rev. 13:17), and so may not "*remain alive in time of famine*". For Catholics like these, "*the thoughts of His Heart*" are a dead letter…

Indeed, for those timid Catholics the problem is simplicity itself: '*How am I ever going to cope under Antichrist?*' And so also is their answer: '*Give in. Submit*'. It is a clear repeat of Adam's problem: 'How am I ever going to cope with a fallen wife?' And of Adam's solution: 'Give in to her. Submit'. Without a thought for prayer or turning to God. And from the effects of Adam's *Original Sin* we may learn, as a valuable lesson for all the lukewarm Catholics of our days, that the way he saw the problem and its solution <u>was far from simple</u>. For it tied him in a terrible knot: "*the knot of Eve*" (Vatican II), as well as in dire punishments from which there was no escape. As Scripture says it so clearly for our times:

> "A third Angel followed, shouting aloud, 'All those who worshipped the beast and its statue, <u>or had themselves branded on the hand or the forehead</u>, will be made to drink the wine of God's fury, which is ready, undiluted, in His cup of anger.....There will be no respite, night or day, for those who worshipped the beast or its

statue or accepted branding with its name'." (Rev. 14:9-11).

Seen in this Light, their 'solution' is far from simple. Obviously it is far more preferable 'to let God do the fighting'. This brings us to intrepid Catholics with their trust in God and in the Promises of the Sacred Heart. To them the 'problem' is not: "*How are we going to cope under Antichrist*", but is put far more simple like this: '*How is Antichrist going to cope with us?*' For, if it is put in this way, they have turned tables on the beast by forcing it to cope with their God. As Scripture says:

> "They [that is, the worldly rulers and their Modernist advisers] are all of one mind in putting their strength and their powers at the disposal of the beast, and they will go to war against the Lamb. But the Lamb is *the Lord of lords and the King of kings*, and He will defeat them. And they will be defeated by His followers, the called, the elect, the faithful ones." (Rev. 17:13-14).

> "This is why the Saints must have constancy and Faith." (Rev. 13:10).

And again:

> "This is why there must be constancy in the Saints who keep the commandments of God and Faith in Jesus." (Rev. 14:12).

For 400 years the Sacred Heart has been encouraging this constancy in Its most trusted servants in preparation for the terrible upheavals in these last times.

That God remembers His faithful servants and their constancy in their hour of need, and feeds them 'in times of famine', can be learned from Sacred Scripture:

> "They threw Daniel into the lion pit and there he stayed for six days. In the pit were seven lions which were given two human bodies and two sheep every day; but for this period they were not given anything to make sure they would eat Daniel.

> Now the prophet Habakkuk was in Judea; he had been making a stew and breaking up bread to put in a basket. He was on his way to the fields, taking this to the harvesters, when the Angel of the Lord spoke to him: 'Take the meal you are carrying to Babylon and give it to Daniel in the lion pit'. 'Lord', replied Habakkuk, 'I have never seen Babylon and know nothing about the pit'. The Angel of the Lord seized him by the top of his head and carried him off by the hair to Babylon where, by the force of his spirit, he set Habakkuk down on the edge of the pit. 'Daniel, Daniel', Habakkuk shouted, 'take the meal that God has sent you'. And Daniel said: 'You have kept me in mind, O God, you have not deserted those who love You'. And rising to his feet he ate the meal, while the Angel of God lost no time in returning Habakkuk to his own country."

"*You have kept me in mind, O God*". Compare this with "*The thoughts of His Heart last through every generation....*". But then, Scripture tells us, Daniel had served his God faithfully in exile in the hostile environment of fickle kings, jealous princes, false priests, career-seeking court officials and the like. He was fearless, but never over-bearing or imprudent in his trust in God, *always knowing what was right and good....*

And then there is the well-known story of the prophet Elijah and the widow of Zarepta which Our Lord held up to the Jews of His time as a warning for their unbelief.

> "There were many widows in Israel, I can assure you, in Elijah's day, when heaven remained shut for three years and six months, and a great famine raged throughout the land, but Elijah was not sent to one of these. He was sent to a widow at Zarepta, a Sidonian town". (Luke 4:25-26).

It was very dicey, in fact it was utter folly, for renegade people to cross swords with Elijah. Twice he destroyed by fire from heaven a captain and his fifty men, sent out by the king of Israel to capture him, so great had become the arrogance and unbelief of leaders and people. Here then is the story of how Elijah *was kept alive* in the three-and-a-half year drought he himself had called down from heaven over his wayward people.

> "Elijah the Tishbite, of Tishbe in Gilead, said to (king) Ahab: 'As Yahweh lives, the God of Israel whom I serve, there shall be neither dew nor rain these years except at my order'.
>
> The word of Yahweh came to him: 'Go away from here, go east-wards, and hide yourself in the wadi of Cherith which lies east of the Jordan. You can drink from the stream and I have given orders to the ravens to bring you food there'. He did as Yahweh had said; he went and stayed in the wadi Cherith. The ravens brought him bread in the morning and meat in the evening, and he quenched his thirst from the stream. But after a while the stream dried up, for the country had no rain. And then the word of Yahweh came to him: 'Up, and go to Zarepta, a Sidonian town, and stay there. I have ordered a widow there to give you food'. So he went off to Sidon. And when he reached the city gate, there was a widow gathering sticks. Addressing her he said: 'Please bring a little water in a vessel for me to

> drink'. She was setting off to bring it when he called after her: 'Please bring me a scrap of bread in your hand'.'As Yahweh your God lives', she replied, 'I have no baked bread'....But Elijah said to her: 'Do not be afraid.....for thus Yahweh speaks, the God of Israel: "The jar of meal shall not be spent, and the jug of oil not be emptied, before the day when Yahweh sends rain on the face of the earth".' (1 Kings, 17:1-14).

"*Do not be afraid....*" Elijah of course was an exceptional man but that should not prevent us from trusting his and our God just as he did. The widow of Zarepta was not of his Faith, but she shared the rewards contained in his. And so will it be with us.

In context we can also point to the twofold feeding of the thousands by Our Lord as contained in the four Gospels, as a reward for following Him to that lonely place. At least one of the Evangelists specifically mentions that the miracle was performed *lest the people would succumb on the way home.* There is ample reason then to put all our trust in the Sacred Heart of Our Blessed Lord *that He will keep us alive in famine*, even miraculously, after we have served Him fearlessly in the face of the hostile Modernists.

That a severe famine is being deliberately prepared by the forerunners of Antichrist is of great concern to the poor of this world. The forebodings are truly ominous. The main cause for anxiety is the worldwide enforcement by the so-called 'rich' countries and their Governments of *genetically modified* (GM) food at the expense of organically grown food. GM grains are being made sterile, so farmers can no longer do what has been an age-old practice: to sell two-thirds of their crop and sow the remaining one-third the next year. They are forced to buy sterile GM grains from GM outlets at monopolistic prices which the Third World farmers cannot afford. Thus their land gets sold and they lose their livelihood.

The world's supermarkets are already stocked with GM food products which cannot be recognised by the customers because the GM food producers are ***not*** requested to label their products so as to facilitate the deception. The whole set-up is an overt and shameless preparation *for buying and selling* *under conditions*, one of which has been mentioned in the Bible as '*the mark of the beast*'.

So, while there is still time, let us love, revere and implore the Sacred Heart in numerous Holy Communions *lest we too succumb on the way to our eternal Home* to the combined forces of Modernism ('the second beast') and Antichrist ('the first beast'). According to the Book of Revelation, "*the second beast will do everything in its power to subjugate the whole world to the tyranny of the first beast.*" (Rev. 13:12).

"I love those who love Me.
And those who wait early at My door
shall gain access to Me.
With Me are riches and honour,
enduring wealth and Divine favour.
My Fruit is better than gold, yes, even the purest,
Better than the finest silver My return.
I walk in the way of virtue, in the paths of justice,
Enriching those who love Me,
filling their treasuries…."

(Book of Proverbs, 8:17-21)

No cause for alarm here. As we already know, Wisdom (speaking here) is personified by both Our Lady and the Holy Catholic Church of which She is the beginning. And the Fruit mentioned here is what this Part II is all about.

A Great Love for the Catholic Church

One of these Fruits of the Holy Catholic Mass is just as hard to find in these troubled times as it is to gather and to keep: ***a great love for the Catholic Church.***

The greatest Object of the love of all the Saints was Christ crucified, Our Lord maltreated, tortured, cursed, abandoned, rejected. Which means of course that they could not find a greater joy and satisfaction than to share in some way this Sacred Passion and Death in their own life's circumstances. But inseparable from this first love was their combined love for the Blessed Virgin Mary and the Holy Catholic Church, the two means by which all their knowledge of Christ and all His graces had come to them. Here the reader is referred to the Epilogue of

Part I of this book where enough has been said of this love for the Catholic Church.

The spectacle of an orthodox Catholic in our modem society is truly a sorry one. No one resembles more the suffering Christ than he does. No one is closer to Our Lady of Sorrows than she is. From the four corners of the globe we hear the same reports: how misunderstood and mistrusted they are by their own bishops and priests, shunned and ignored by fellow Catholics who have followed the *winds of change* and no longer share their beliefs; how they are treated with impatience and contempt by the catechists, who go through the motions of pretending to teach their children the catechism, and how disobeyed they are by their own teenage sons and daughters: the products of this teaching.

Redress by their bishops is denied them; the road to the parish priest is blocked; they are unable to get a hearing in the 'catholic' press; Sister and Curate are altogether on another wavelength, and the few words they manage to utter at parents meetings are drowned in a torrent of modern jargon, spiced with derision and intolerance.

To add to their daily agony, what do they see? They see a renewal which has been cleverly hijacked and twisted into some unrecognisable shape, which bears no resemblance to what was originally intended. They see bishops silent in the face of a monstrous perversion of Catholic doctrine. They see the seminaries empty. They see their Priests and Nuns leave the Church and leave Catholic education. They see teenagers refuse to attend Mass on Sundays, and adopt practices contrary to Catholic teaching. They see apostates and atheists appointed to catholic schools as teachers in compliance with some spurious 'anti-discrimination laws'. They see their children come out of 'catholic schools' with hardly any knowledge of their Faith and with barely the rudiments of morality, all in the name of some 'renewal'. To say nothing of what they read in their catholic papers, or hear from the pulpit, or in the never ending seminars and gatherings, where it is all explained to them that this 'renewal' comes from Vatican II, and must be seen as the work of 'the Spirit', who is preparing us for some united, ecumenical church of the future.

And then it is finally brought home to them that the only thing that stands in the way of this renewal is they themselves. They are the obstinate obstacles, the cross of the bishops, the bone of contention in parish life: the splitters, the wreckers, the cause of divisions. They must constantly show cause for their existence, for their Faith; all the others have it made. Their opposition to Modernism is suspect: the intolerance of Modernism to them is claimed to come from 'the Spirit' and is taken for granted.

It is obvious to friend and foe alike, that this situation cannot go on indefinitely. Sooner or later one camp will prevail over the other. One camp will show to have Supernatural Faith, Hope and Love on its side, the Communion of Saints, the Catholic Church. That camp will first suffer apparent defeat, and rejection, like Christ had to go through. And to sustain that camp through the agony of defeat and rejection, before it can take heart in the final victory, God has given to His camp one thing and one thing only that the opposite camp never can claim and will never possess, and that is *truth*. Finally, when all is said and done, when it no longer matters who had the ear of the bishops, who had the parish priest in their pocket, who had the numbers, who monopolised the catholic press, who could lay hands on unlimited sums of money for their propaganda: the deciding factor is: who is in the company of the same Jesus who divinely revealed before Pilate, that He had come into this world to testify to the Truth, and that all who are of the Truth would hear His voice. For Truth and Christ are synonymous, are one and the same, as He himself told us: "I am the Truth".

A Great Love for the Light of Catholic Faith

With this we have come across yet another Fruit of the Catholic Mass: <u>a great love for the Light of Catholic Faith</u> in which Jesus' Truth is seen and recognised, and a great respect for the faculty in man, the human mind, that contains this Supernaturally infused Light, recognises the Truth, and makes it its own.

For well over one hundred years our Holy Mother the Catholic Church has been warning us that the Enemy has been concentrating his attacks on the Catholic Faith. This attack has become very refined, and subtle and brutal. Everywhere in the world our good Catholics are being put under an almost intolerable pressure to hand over their Catholic Faith in exchange for a teilhardian, modernist persuasion, which is being proclaimed as the new Catholicism ensuing from Vatican II, in line with modern, evolutionary trends. It is the purpose of this little book to alleviate this pressure, help to put a stop to this by showing every catholic reader what it is they are asked so insistently and relentlessly to surrender.

The more we grow in love for our God-given Catholic Faith by frequent Mass attendance, the more we will come to see in its Light that Catholic Faith is, in a real sense, undoubtedly the most precious gift of Almighty God to finite little man here on earth. For, although nothing could surpass in greatness the Gift of Himself in the Blessed Eucharist, where on earth is this Gift accepted and appreciated other than by a lively Catholic Faith? And the same goes for all the other Holy Realities revealed by God and given to us: Our Lady, the Sacraments, the Catholic Church itself: all only seen and appreciated in the Supernatural Light of Catholic Faith.

> (1) Now faith is the assurance of things hoped for, the conviction of things not seen. (2) For by it the men of old received divine approval. (3) By faith we understand that the world was created by the word of God, so that what is seen was made out of things which do not appear. (4) By faith Abel offered to God a more acceptable sacrifice than Cain, through which he received approval as righteous, God bearing witness by accepting his gifts; he died, but through his faith he is still speaking. (5) By faith Enoch was taken up so that he should not see death; and he was not found, because God had taken him. Now before he was taken he was attested as having pleased God. (6) And without faith it is impossible to please him. For whoever would draw near to God must believe that he exists and that he rewards those who seek him. (7) By faith Noah, being warned by God concerning events as yet unseen, took heed and constructed an ark for the saving of his household; by this he con-

demned the world and became an heir of the righteousness which comes by faith. (8) By faith Abraham obeyed when he was called to go out to a place which he was to receive as an inheritance; and he went out, not knowing where he was to go. (9) By faith he sojourned in the land of promise, as in a foreign land, living in tents with Isaac and Jacob, heirs with him of the same promise. (10) For he looked forward to the city which has foundations, whose builder and maker is God. (11) By faith Sarah herself received power to conceive, even when she was past the age, since she considered him faithful who had promised. (12) Therefore from one man, and him as good as dead, were born descendants as many as the stars of heaven and as the innumerable grains of sand by the seashore. (13) These all died in faith, not having received what was promised, but having seen it and greeted it from afar, and having acknowledged that they were strangers and exiles on the earth. (14) For people who speak thus make it clear that they are seeking a homeland. (15) If they had been thinking of that land from which they had gone out, they would have had opportunity to return. (16) But as it is, they desire a better country, that is, a heavenly one. Therefore God is not ashamed to be called their God, for he has prepared for them a city. (17) By faith Abraham, when he was tested, offered up Isaac, and he who had received the promises was ready to offer up his only son, (18) of whom it was said, "Through Isaac shall your descendants be named." (19) He considered that God was able to raise men even from the dead; hence, figuratively speaking, he did receive him back. (20) By faith Isaac invoked future blessings on Jacob and Esau. (21) By faith Jacob, when dying, blessed each of the sons of Joseph, bowing in worship over the head of his staff. (22) By faith Joseph, at the end of his life, made mention of the exodus of the Israelites and gave directions concerning his burial. (23) By faith Moses, when he was born, was hid for three months by his parents, because they saw that the child was beautiful; and they were not afraid of the king's edict. (24) By faith Moses, when he was grown up, refused to be called the son of Pharaoh's daughter, (25) choosing rather to share ill-treatment with the people of God than to enjoy the fleeting pleasures of sin. (26) He considered abuse suffered for the Christ greater wealth than the treasures of Egypt, for he looked to the reward. (27) By faith he left Egypt, not being afraid of the anger of the king; for he endured as seeing him who is invisible. (28) By faith he kept the Passover and sprinkled the blood, so that the Destroyer of the first-born might not touch them. (29) By faith the people crossed the Red Sea as if on dry land; but the Egyptians, when they attempted to do the same, were drowned. (30) By faith the walls of Jericho fell down after they had been encircled for seven days. (31) By faith Rahab the harlot did not perish with those who were disobedient, because she had given friendly welcome to the spies. (32) And what more shall I say? For time would fail me to tell of Gideon, Barak, Samson, Jephthah, of David and Samuel and the prophets, (33) who through faith conquered kingdoms, enforced justice, received promises, stopped the mouths of lions, (34) quenched raging fire, escaped the edge of the sword, won strength out of weak-

> ness, became mighty in war, put foreign armies to flight. (35) Women received their dead by resurrection. Some were tortured, refusing to accept release, that they might rise again to a better life. (36) Others suffered mocking and scourging, and even chains and imprisonment. (37) They were stoned, they were sawn in two, they were killed with the sword; they went about in skins of sheep and goats, destitute, afflicted, ill-treated, (38) of whom the world was not worthy, wandering over deserts and mountains, and in dens and caves of the earth. (39) And all these, though well attested by their faith, did not receive what was promised, (40) since God had foreseen something better for us, that apart from us they should not be made perfect. (Hebr. 11:1-40)

Is what the cold, lukewarm, worldly, pleasure-seeking and yes, even apostate Catholics of our days have to offer to God really ***better*** than what these heroes of the Faith had to give to the Almighty? Are they truly *making them perfect*, they, who have received all that the Cross of Christ and the Holy Sacrifice of the Mass have won for us, but are no longer seeking it? How harder it will be on Judgement Day for those who received everything that the New Testament has to offer, and could not even equal, let alone surpass, the Faith of those of the Old Testament described here by St. Paul.

We will meet these Saints again in the next episode.

A Great Love for the Communion of Saints: the Kingdom of God

Because of the almost unanimous decision taken by the Fathers of the Second Vatican Council ***not*** to issue a separate Decree on Our Lady, but to treat Her as an integral part of the Mystery of the Church at this time of great trial and tribulation, the children of Mary will clearly see the Great Lady ***in*** the Church, and the Church ***in*** Our Lady. And their filial devotion for the Mother of God will become inseparable from their great love for the Church.

It is truly amazing to see so many Catholics, who have survived "cyclone Teilhard", who successfully withstood the onslaughts of Modernism, who have no time for false apparitions, but kept untrammelled their childlike Catholic Faith, are found to have a singular devotion to Our Lady, and more specifically are greatly devoted to Our Lady of Fatima. The devout wearing of Her Sacred Scapular has re-enacted for them the wondrous protection by the Angel of God, who descended with the three young men in the burning, fiery furnace of king Nabuchadnezar, making the inside of this raging furnace bearable to live in. (Dan. 3:4-50).

Our first concern is the *Kingdom of God*, Our Holy Catholic Church, the Mystical Body of Christ, which, as we know, is ***in*** this world but not ***of*** this world. The grave injunction of Our Lady at Fatima: to be concerned for sinners and for the avoidance of sin, as well as for the reparation of sin, is a 20th century reminder of Her Son's command to us:

> "Set Your hearts on His Kingdom first, and on its righteousness, and all these other things will be given to you as well." (Mat.6:33).

Long before Teilhard's fancies were openly preached within the confines of the 'City of God', affluent Western Catholics had become ashamed of being identified with simple people whose first concern was the spiritual Kingdom of God; and so it came about that this concern was left to the Saints, or to 'religious fanatics and cranks'. Self-respecting Catholics became self-conscious about their religious practices and fervour; and the 'childlike faith' as demanded by Our Lord's solemn warning: "*Truly I say to you: unless you change and become like little children, you will never enter the Kingdom of Heaven*" got lost. (Mat. 18 3). This abandonment of the concern for the Kingdom of God, and the grateful acceptance of the fortuitous teilhardian substitute of 'Building the earth', has been hailed everywhere as a sign of Catholic maturity, of which the reception of Communion in the hand has become both the symbol and the excess. And with their exodus from the Catholic Church it became clear to those who remained *in their Father's House* how Catholics lose contact with Our Blessed Lady and are unable to see Her in the various 'churches' that are being presented to them.

- She is ***not*** found in the "One-World Church" depicted by Pope St. Pius X, a truly

Modernist monstrosity with no discipline of the mind, no curb on the passions, no hierarchy, no dogma, intent to bring back to the world the reign of legalised cunning, and brute force, and the oppression of the weak and of all those who toil and suffer.

- She is ***not*** found in the 'religious movement' of the second Beast doing everything in its power to subjugate the whole world to the tyranny of the first Beast. A true parallel description of what Pope St. Pius X saw and outlined in more detail.
- She is ***not*** found in a 'church' where God has been allocated by Teilhard de Chardin His place: that of the 'soul of evolution', in which 'church' evolution will from then on take care of everything.
- She is ***not*** found in "*Building the earth*" in which, even if proposed as a 'church', Her Son will never find His '*divine milieu*'.
- She is ***not*** found in the 'churches' that broke away from the Catholic Church during and since the Protestant Reformation in the 16th

century and have now regrouped themselves in *The World Council of Churches*.

- Finally, She is ***not*** found in any of the 'Catholic sub-cultures' which have sprung up out of disobedience against legitimate Church authority: groupings formed around the spate of false 'apparitions' which were condemned by the bishops of the various dioceses in which they were supposed to have occurred.

We may gauge from the throngs of Catholics who have flocked worldwide to one or another of these above-mentioned agglomerates, how serious the loss of their cohesion has become away from the Mother Church, the only one where Mary can be seen ***in*** the Church and the Church ***in*** the Mother of God. In times like these great strength and consolation are given to Catholics who, under the impulses of grace, turn to the Lives of the Saints to see how they served their God and their Church and how to be inspired by the ways in which they overcame their difficulties and turned apparent defeat into victories for the Lamb of God.

To be thoroughly at home in *The Communion of Saints*, that spiritual intercourse between the Blessed in Heaven, the faithful on earth and the Holy Souls in purgatory, is a great Fruit of the Holy Sacrifice of the Mass as well as being a Dogma of the Catholic Church and an article of Faith in the Creed. The roots of this Sacred Tradition go back to the Old Testament. Vatican II, sensing strongly the corrupting influence of an earth-centered substitute for the Catholic Faith, has stressed with unusual emphasis the overriding importance of this Dogma in her Dogmatic Constitution on the Church, *Lumen Gentium*, Ch, 7. There is rich material here, and the reader is referred to this section for enlightenment in the traditional teachings of the Church on this topic.

Out of the legacy which he Saints have left us from their lives in their work for the Church in fighting *sin* and all the evils of their day that flowed from it: *ignorance*, *error* and the *corruption of doctrine*, we must learn how to deal with the consequences of sin in our own times. And this great gift of knowing and applying this so necessary *Catholic resourcefulness* in the Communion of Saints is obtained in frequent Mass attendance and Holy Communion. The world is full of books of the Lives of the Saints, and it is a great consolation to know that God will never refuse us access to these if we ask Him for it.

> "Set your hearts on His Kingdom first, and on its righteousness, and all these other things will be given to you as well." (Mat. 6:33).

> "Truly I say to you: unless you change and become like little children, you will never enter the Kingdom of Heaven." (Mat. 18 3).

It is here, as I said we would, that we meet up again with the Heroes of the Faith as depicted by St. Paul in his Letter to the Hebrews. If they were such an inspiration for the Apostle of the Gentiles, so should they, and all the Saints in the New Covenant, be for us. And after two thousand years of Christianity we have even more justification than St. Paul had to apply to ourselves the words which this great Apostle used to conclude this part of his Letter:

"Surrounded then on every side by this great cloud of witnesses we too should throw off everything that hinders us, especially the sin that clings so easily, and keep running steadily in the race we have started. Let us not lose sight of Jesus who leads us in our Faith and brings it to perfection. For the sake of the joy that was still in the future He endured the Cross, disregarding the shamefulness of it, and from now on has taken his place at the right of God's throne. Think of the way he stood such opposition from sinners, and then you will not give up for want of courage. In the fight against sin you have not yet had to keep fighting to the point of death." (Hebr. 12:1-4).

"How blessed are the poor in spirit,
the Kingdom of Heaven is theirs.
Blessed are the gentle,
They shall have the earth for their heritage.
Blessed are those who mourn,
They shall be comforted.
Blessed are those who hunger and thirst
for what is right,

They shall be satisfied.
Blessed the merciful,
They shall have mercy shown them.
Blessed the pure of heart,
They shall see God.
Blessed are the peacemakers,
They shall be called the sons of God.
Blessed are those who are persecuted
for the cause of right,
Theirs is the Kingdom of Heaven."

It would be difficult to find a better way to finish this section on the Fruits of the Holy Catholic Mass than with the Eight Beatitudes, which the Son of God has laid at the foundation of the Kingdom of His Father both in time and in eternity.

And if one of these is to be singled out, then we must say that seven of them form the crown in which is set the pearl of great beauty: '*purity of heart*'. Those who possess that jewel '*see God*'. They see God's Hand in all that happens here on earth, and they will see Him in a very special way for all eternity.

www.ingramcontent.com/pod-product-compliance
Lightning Source LLC
LaVergne TN
LVHW040220110826
845146LV00005B/1355

* 9 7 9 8 8 8 8 7 0 5 2 8 5 *